LOVE AT FIRST BITE

THE COMPLETE
VAMPIRE LOVER'S
COOKBOOK

MICHELLE ROY KELLY
& ANDREA NORVILLE

Adamsmedia

AVON, MASSACHUSETTS

Published by
Adams Media, a division of F+W Media, Inc.
57 Littlefield Street, Avon, MA 02322. U.S.A.
www.adamsmedia.com

ISBN 10: 1-4405-0358-3
ISBN 13: 978-1-4405-0358-0
eISBN 10: 1-4405-0705-8
eISBN 13: 978-1-4405-0705-2

Printed in the United States of America.

10 9 8 7 6 5 4 3 2 1

Library of Congress Cataloging-in-Publication Data
is available from the publisher.

This publication is designed to provide accurate and authoritative information with regard to the subject matter covered. It is sold with the understanding that the publisher is not engaged in rendering legal, accounting, or other professional advice. If legal advice or other expert assistance is required, the services of a competent professional person should be sought.

—From a *Declaration of Principles* jointly adopted by a Committee of the American Bar Association and a Committee of Publishers and Associations

Many of the designations used by manufacturers and sellers to distinguish their product are claimed as trademarks. Where those designations appear in this book and Adams Media was aware of a trademark claim, the designations have been printed with initial capital letters.

Disclaimer: Although garlic is known to be a vampire repellent, in the interest of flavor, many of the recipes in this cookbook include this ingredient.

Heart and crown image © istock/sx70.

This book is available at quantity discounts for bulk purchases.
For information, please call 1-800-289-0963.

DEDICATION

For my husband Michael and my favorite ankle biters,
Meredith and Genevieve. — M.R.K.

This one is for my little vampire family—Jonny, Maddy,
and Teeny—my creatures of the night. — A.N.

ACKNOWLEDGMENTS

A big shout out to everyone who helped on this project—the
waitress who sparked the idea; Andrea for her enthusiasm and
writing, Michael for his support, advice, and suggestions; Sue for
making the numbers work; Meredith Sr. for listening to the rav-
ings of a mad woman; and Matt for those truly inspired recipe
names and his expansive trivial knowledge. — M.R.K.

Many, many thanks to Michelle for letting me collaborate on
such a great idea—it was so much fun!; my family for their love
and tasting my creations, and everyone at Adams for their hard
work and support. — A.N.

CONTENTS

Introduction

Greetings mortals! In your hands, you hold the key to all your feasting fantasies. This collection of fangtastic food and drink will take you on a nightmarish culinary adventure you won't soon forget.

The traditional vampire's diet is highly predictable and boring. Blood, blood, and more blood. The mortal palatte is harder to please. Inside these pages you will find more than 300 blood-suckingly good recipes to share with family and friends. While these scrumptious recipes are for mere mortals, they are inspired by the passion, intrigue, and mystery of our favorite—and likewise ravenous—creatures of the night.

So, put on your apron, dim the lights, and get ready for some devilish delights!

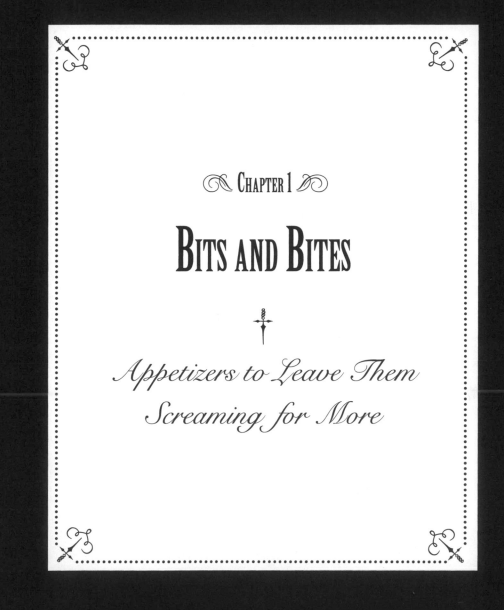

CHAPTER 1

BITS AND BITES

Appetizers to Leave Them Screaming for More

Bo Peep Bites

Serves 12

4 pounds boned leg of lamb, cut into 1" cubes
1 cup olive oil
½ cup lemon juice or red wine vinegar
1 tablespoon Worcestershire sauce
4 cloves garlic, minced
1 onion, coarsely chopped
¼ cup dried rosemary leaves
1 tablespoon dried oregano
Salt and black pepper to taste

Place lamb cubes in a large, resealable plastic bag.

Combine olive oil, lemon juice or red wine vinegar , Worcestershire sauce, garlic, onion, rosemary, and oregano. Mix well and pour into bag over lamb cubes. Seal well.

Place on a platter and refrigerate 8 hours or overnight, turning bag occasionally.

Remove from refrigerator, drain off marinade, and push lamb cubes onto skewers. Sprinkle with salt and black pepper.

Cook on a grill over medium-high heat for 15 minutes, turning frequently. Push lamb from skewers onto a platter and serve.

Love at First Bite

Scorched Tuna Bites

Serves 12

6 (1"-thick) sushi-grade tuna steaks
½ cup vegetable oil
2 tablespoons sesame oil
½ cup maple syrup
⅓ cup soy sauce
2 tablespoons fresh ginger, grated
⅓ cup lemon juice
Black pepper to taste
Sesame seeds

Place tuna steaks in a baking pan. Combine ⅓ cup vegetable oil (reserve remaining), sesame oil, maple syrup, soy sauce, ginger, and lemon juice. Pour over steaks.

Refrigerate and let marinate for 30 minutes, turning once.

Pour remaining oil into a skillet over high heat.

Remove steaks from marinade and drain. Sprinkle with black pepper. Sear each steak for 2 minutes on each side.

Cut seared steaks into 1" cubes, sprinkle with sesame seeds, and serve immediately.

Awful Fond of You Falafel Fondue
Serves 6

2 cups chickpeas, soaked overnight
1 onion, finely chopped
¼ cup fresh parsley, minced
¼ cup cilantro, minced
2 cloves garlic, pressed
1 teaspoon baking powder
½ teaspoon cumin
¼ teaspoon sesame oil
Salt and pepper to taste
5 cups peanut oil or combination vegetable and olive oil
Tahini

Drain chickpeas. Place in a food processor with onion, parsley, cilantro, and garlic. Pulse a few times.

Add baking powder, cumin, sesame oil, salt, and pepper. Pulse until mixture forms a smooth paste.

Roll paste into firm 1" balls.

Heat oil in one or more fondue pots, taking care not to fill pots more than ⅓ full. Guests can use fondue forks to skewer firm falafel balls, or use wire strainers to dip falafel in hot oil.

Cook until balls are brown and crisp. Dip in tahini before eating.

Love at First Bite

Bloody Mary Fondue
Serves 8

6 cups tomato or mixed vegetable juice
⅔ cup vodka
Juice of 2 limes
Juice of 1 lemon
½ cup horseradish
1 tablespoon Tabasco sauce
1 tablespoon Worcestershire sauce
2 bay leaves

In a large saucepan, whisk together all ingredients until well blended. Bring to a boil. Reduce heat and simmer for 3 minutes.

Pour into 1 or more fondue pots. Place pot over heat source and serve with vegetable platter and 7-grain bread cubes.

TASTY TIDBIT

FOR THE VAMPIRES OF FOLKLORE, DIETS RANGE FROM BLOOD TO THE FLESH OF BOTH HUMANS AND CORPSES AND A WIDE RANGE OF HUMAN ORGANS, BIRTH-RELATED MATTER, AND OTHER NASTIES SUCH AS ENTRAILS.

Manhunt Nachos

Serves 4–6

1 can sloppy joe sauce
1 pound ground beef or ground turkey
1 bag tortilla chips
⅓ cup Velveeta cheese sauce, warmed
⅓ cup salsa, warmed
Sour cream, for dipping

Prepare sloppy joe sauce and ground beef or turkey according to label directions.

Spread chips on a platter and smother with sloppy joe mixture.

Drizzle with cheese sauce and salsa. Serve with sour cream on the side.

TASTY TIDBIT

ONE OF THE FIRST VAMPIRE CASES IN THE UNITED STATES WAS THAT OF MERCY BROWN IN EXETER, RHODE ISLAND. AFTER THE DEATH OF BRAM STOKER, NEWSPAPER ACCOUNTS OF THE EXHUMATION OF MERCY BROWN'S BODY WERE FOUND AMONG HIS PAPERS AND NOTES.

Love at First Bite

Naughty Pillows in Burgundy Fondue
Serves 8

2 pounds shrimp, cooked
1 pound andouille sausage, chopped
1 pound ham, diced
1 cup green onion, sliced
1 cup red bell pepper, diced
3–5 cups of burgundy
3 bay leaves

Cut shrimp in half.

Lay out 32 2" squares of cheesecloth. Divide shrimp, sausage, ham, green onion, and bell pepper among the squares. Bring ends of squares together and tie with string to make closed pouches.

Bring burgundy to a boil in a saucepan and add bay leaves. Pour burgundy into one or more fondue pots and place pot over heating source.

Guests can lift pillows into wine with forks, small tongs, or strainers. Purses should be left in the fondue just until ingredients are warmed and flavored. After, ingredients should be removed from cheesecloth onto plates.

Yield: 1 loaf

1 tablespoon active dry yeast
½ cup warm water
5 eggs
1 tablespoon aniseed
¼ cup butter
½ cup sugar
½ teaspoon salt
½ teaspoon ground nutmeg
2½ cups flour

Preheat oven to 375°F. Dissolve yeast in ¼ cup warm water. Separate 2 eggs. Beat together 2 eggs plus 2 egg yolks. Steep aniseed in remaining ¼ cup warm water for 10 to 15 minutes. Melt butter in a small saucepan on low heat.

Put the yeast water and 1 tablespoon sugar in a large mixing bowl. Stir gently. Let sit about 10 minutes or until it appears foamy.

Stir in salt, ⅓ cup sugar, nutmeg, melted butter, aniseed with water, and the beaten eggs and yolks. Mix well while slowly adding 2½ cups flour. The dough should be slightly sticky. Knead for 10 to 15 minutes.

Lightly coat a large mixing bowl with oil or shortening. Place dough inside and cover with a towel. Place in a warm location and let rise until doubled, usually 1 to 2 hours.

Punch the dough down and place it on a floured surface. Remove a handful of dough and set aside. Shape remaining dough into a round loaf about 1" thick and place it on a greased cookie sheet.

Make a deep indentation in the center of the loaf with your fist. Form the small piece of dough set aside into two "bone" shapes about 4" long and one "skull" shape. Place these in the center indentation.

Cover the dough with a towel and place in a warm location to rise for 45 minutes to 1 hour. The dough should hold a finger-print when pressed.

Bake for 30 minutes or until golden brown.

Beat remaining egg and use it as a wash on the bread while the bread is still warm. Sprinkle with remaining sugar.

TASTY TIDBIT

Los Dias de Los Muertos or the Days of the Dead are a holiday time when Mexicans celebrate the return of the souls of their departed loved ones. It is a time of celebration with memorial altars set up for the dead souls who will, according to the tradition, be streaming through tears in the veil between the worlds to visit their families and have a brief taste of living once again. Their favorite foods and trinkets decorate the altars, and families pack up baskets of holiday foods, candles, flowers, and tequila to picnic at the gravesides of their loved ones. Though it may sound somber to those from other traditions, this is actually a very festive, happy holiday.

Blood Oranges and My Darling Clementines
Serves 4

2 blood oranges
1 teaspoon rose water
¼ cup pomegranate seeds
2 clementines or mandarin oranges

Slice the tops and bottoms off the blood oranges and set them on one of the cut surfaces.

With a sharp knife, cut the peel and pith off the oranges in downward strips around each orange to reveal the flesh. Cut the oranges into thin slices across the width, making round wheel slices. Remove any seeds.

Arrange the orange slices on four plates and sprinkle the rose water over them. Sprinkle the pomegranate seeds over the slices.

Peel the clementines and separate them into individual sections. Scatter the sections onto the blood oranges, dividing them among the four plates.

Love at First Bite

Louis's Down-Home Praline Pecans

Serves 4

1 tablespoon heavy cream
1 tablespoon dark rum
¼ teaspoon Tabasco sauce
1 cup pecan halves
¼ cup brown sugar

Preheat oven to 350°F.

Combine the cream, rum, and Tabasco in a bowl. Add the pecans and stir to coat. Add the brown sugar and toss with a fork to coat the pecans.

Pour the coated pecans onto a baking sheet lined with nonstick foil and separate them into individual nuts with a fork.

Bake for 10 minutes, stir the nuts around, and bake another 5 minutes. Let cool on the foil and then store in a tin with a tight-fitting lid.

TASTY TIDBIT

IN ANNE RICE'S *INTERVIEW WITH THE VAMPIRE*, WE MEET LOUIS DE POINTE DU LAC, ARGUABLY THE MOST TORTURED VAMPIRE EVER CREATED. HE WAS SO CONFLICTED ABOUT TAKING A HUMAN LIFE THAT HE FED ON RATS AND DOVES TO SURVIVE.

Shallow Grave Shallot Tart
Serves 4

2 tablespoons unsalted butter, softened
6 shallots, peeled
1 teaspoon salt
¼ teaspoon pepper
½ teaspoon dried thyme
1 sheet frozen puff pastry, thawed
2 tablespoons chopped fresh chives

Preheat oven to 400°F. Spread the soft butter over the bottom of an 8" × 8" glass dish.

Slice the shallots into ¼"-thick slices and arrange them in the dish, cut-side down, in one layer. Sprinkle them with salt, pepper, and thyme.

Unfold the puff pastry and cut it into a square that will fit in the dish. Prick the pastry all over with a fork. Put the pastry on top of the shallots and tuck the pastry down in the dish.

Bake for 15 minutes, reduce heat to 325°F, and continue baking for 30 minutes.

Remove the dish from the oven and put a cookie sheet over it. Flip the dish over onto the cookie sheet and carefully remove it. The tart will be on the cookie sheet. Cut it into four squares and serve sprinkled with chives.

Love at First Bite

Immortal Gyro Bites

Serves 4–6

¼ pound ground beef
¼ pound ground lamb
2 tablespoons minced onion
1 clove garlic, pressed
¼ teaspoon celery salt
½ teaspoon Worcestershire sauce
1 egg white
2 teaspoons chopped fresh parsley
2 teaspoons dried oregano
½ teaspoon black pepper

½ teaspoon salt
2 tablespoons oatmeal
2 tablespoons breadcrumbs
2 teaspoons olive oil
3 pita-bread rounds
½ cup Greek yogurt
Tomatoes
Onions
Lettuce

Preheat oven to 350°F.

Combine all ingredients except the olive oil, pita, Greek yogurt, tomatoes, onions, and lettuce in a bowl with your hands. Shape the mixture into a log and press it into a loaf pan. Brush the top with olive oil.

Bake, uncovered, until thermometer inserted in center reads 160°F, about 1 hour. Let the loaf cool and refrigerate it until ready to use.

Slice the chilled meatloaf thinly and sear the slices in a hot sauté pan. Cut the pita rounds in half to make six pita pockets.

Fill the pockets with seared meat slices and cut each pocket into smaller triangles. Arrange the triangles on a plate and serve with Greek yogurt, tomatoes, onions, and lettuce.

Serves 6

9 eggs
1/4 cup mayonnaise
1 tablespoon mustard, yellow or Dijon
2 tablespoons sour cream (optional)
1 teaspoon salt
1/2 teaspoon pepper
2 teaspoons dried dill weed
1/4 teaspoon cayenne pepper sauce
Paprika

Put the eggs in a saucepan and cover them with water. Bring water to a boil, then reduce heat so that the water is simmering. Set the timer for 15 minutes.

When the timer goes off, pour the hot water out of the saucepan and run cold water over the eggs.

Crack and peel eggs carefully. Cut peeled eggs in half, carefully remove yolks, and set aside white halves. Put yolks in a bowl and mash with a fork.

Add mayonnaise, mustard, and sour cream to yolk mixture and mix together with fork to form a smooth paste, then season with salt, pepper, dill weed, and cayenne pepper sauce.

Scoop about 1 tablespoon of the yolk filling into each white. Cover and refrigerate until chilled.

Sprinkle deviled eggs with paprika before serving.

Serves 6

6 hard-boiled eggs, peeled and cooled
½ cup mayonnaise
1 teaspoon mustard
½ teaspoon garlic salt
Freshly ground pepper to taste
12 small black or green pitted olives, chopped

Cut the peeled eggs in half. Arrange the whites on a plate, scooping the yolks into a bowl. Using an immersion blender, or a fork, beat in the rest of the ingredients, one by one until well blended.

Fill the eggs and either serve immediately or refrigerate, covered.

TASTY TIDBIT

GARLIC HAS A LONG HISTORY OF USE AS A VAMPIRE REPELLENT. LONG BEFORE BRAM STOKER INTRODUCED IT TO READERS IN *DRACULA*, THIS HERB WAS EMPLOYED FOR CENTURIES AROUND THE WORLD AS A PROTECTIVE FORCE AGAINST EVIL SPIRITS OF ALL KINDS.

Beaten and Bruised Brie and Blue Spread

Serves 6

7 ounces Brie cheese, rind removed, at room temperature
2 ounces blue cheese, at room temperature
3 tablespoons butter, at room temperature
¼ cup heavy cream
Freshly ground white pepper, to taste
Parsley sprigs, for garnish

———————— •❖• ————————

Combine the cheeses and butter in a food processor fitted with a metal blade; process the cheese and butter for 10 seconds. Add the cream and pepper, and process until smooth, stopping once to scrape down the sides of the bowl.

Transfer to serving dish and garnish with parsley sprigs. Serve at room temperature. The spread can be prepared up to three days in advance, kept covered and refrigerated. Bring to room temperature before serving.

Tantalizing Trio of Caviar
Serves 4

*2 ounces each: lumpfish caviar, salmon roe,
and golden whitefish caviar
1 lemon, cut into 4 wedges, seeds removed
4 slices of bread, crusts removed and lightly toasted,
cut into triangle quarters
¼ cup crème fraîche or sour cream
4 teaspoons minced white onion
Freshly cracked black pepper, to taste*

Chill 4 salad plates.

Just before you are ready to assemble the appetizer, remove the plates from the refrigerator. Place ½ ounce of each type of caviar on each plate, with each dollop just touching the others on the plate. Place a lemon wedge on each plate.

Stack 4 toast points on each plate and add a dollop of crème fraîche and 1 teaspoon of minced onion. Add a few twists of cracked pepper on the crème fraîche and chill until ready to serve. Each of the plates should look exactly alike for presentation.

Tenderloin Bites with Creamy Horseradish Sauce

Serves 6

¼ cup prepared horseradish
½ cup sour cream
2 (6-ounce) filet mignon steaks
1½ tablespoons olive oil
¼ teaspoon kosher salt
Freshly cracked black pepper, to taste
12 Asian soup spoons
12 toothpicks

In a small bowl, mix together the horseradish and sour cream. Set aside.

Cut each steak into 6 pieces as evenly sized as possible. Transfer to a medium-sized bowl and toss with 1 tablespoon of the olive oil, salt, and pepper until evenly coated.

Heat the remaining ½ tablespoon of olive oil in a nonstick sauté pan over medium-high heat. When very hot, but not smoking, add the beef cubes and sear on each side for about 1 minute per side for rare, about 1½ minutes per side for medium.

Transfer the meat to a plate and tent with tinfoil to keep warm. Let rest for about 7 minutes to allow the juice to reabsorb.

To serve, arrange the spoons on a serving platter. Use a toothpick to spear a piece of meat and place it on one of the spoons; continue with the remaining pieces.

Drizzle any remaining juices over each piece. Add a dollop of the horseradish sauce just to the side of each piece of beef. Serve warm.

Love at First Bite

Swine Bites

Serves 6

1 clove garlic
½ cup fresh basil leaves, stems removed
3 tablespoons olive oil
2 tablespoons shredded Parmesan
3 ounces unflavored mascarpone cheese or cream cheese,
at room temperature
1–2 tablespoons heavy cream
⅛ teaspoon salt
Freshly cracked pepper, to taste
1 pound hot Italian sausage links, cut into 12–18 even-sized pieces
12–18 toothpicks
12–18 Asian soup spoons

———————◆◆◆◆◆———————

Fit the bowl of a food processor with the metal blade. With the motor running, drop the garlic clove through the feed tube. Add the basil, olive oil, and Parmesan, and process until smooth. Add a little more oil if needed. The basil mixture should be a paste-like consistency. Add the mascarpone and process, scraping down the sides of the bowl as needed. With the motor running, add 1 tablespoon of the cream, the salt, and pepper. The pesto should be thick but pourable. Add more cream, little by little, until the proper consistency is achieved. Taste and adjust seasoning as needed. Set aside.

Heat a medium-sized nonstick sauté pan over medium-high heat. Add the sausage pieces and cook, stirring occasionally to prevent sticking. Cover the pan and cook through, about 12 to 14 minutes.

To serve, spear each sausage piece with a toothpick and place it on one of the spoons. Drizzle about 1 teaspoon of the mascarpone pesto over each sausage piece. Serve warm.

Spine-Tingling Beef Bites

Serves 4

2 tablespoons sesame oil
2 tablespoons soy sauce
1 teaspoon fresh ginger, peeled and grated
1 clove garlic, minced
1 teaspoon wasabi powder
2 teaspoons lemon juice
1 tablespoon freshly grated orange rind
1 teaspoon sugar
1 tablespoon fresh cilantro or parsley, minced
Salt and pepper to taste
1 pound lean sirloin, cut in 1" chunks

Whisk all ingredients except the beef in a bowl. When the sauce is well blended, add the sirloin chunks. Marinate for 1 hour.

Heat your grill or broiler to medium high. String the beef on skewers and place on the grill for 8 to 12 minutes, turning frequently, or run the beef under the broiler for four minutes per side.

Love at First Bite

Bloody Mary Aspic and Eggs
Serves 8

¼ cup cold water
½ ounce unflavored gelatin
1 cup boiling tomato juice with no added sugar
2 cups cold tomato juice with no added sugar
1 teaspoon soy sauce
½ teaspoon cayenne pepper, or to taste
Juice of ½ lime
1 teaspoon sugar
1 teaspoon prepared horseradish
Salt and pepper to taste
4 hard-boiled eggs, peeled and halved
8 teaspoons low-fat sour cream for garnish

Place the cold water and gelatin in the bowl of a blender. Let bloom for 3 minutes. Start the motor and slowly add the hot tomato juice, then the cold tomato juice.

With the motor running, pour in the soy sauce, cayenne pepper, lime juice, sugar, horseradish, salt, and pepper. Pour into a 4-cup mold.

Refrigerate for 45 minutes. Insert the hard-boiled eggs into the slightly firm aspic. When completely firm, about 3 hours, turn out on a serving plate.

Spoon sour cream on each serving of this pretty salad.

Elvira's Oysters in the Nude with Three Sauces

1 pound coarse sea salt
2 dozen shucked raw oysters on the half shell
¼ cup red wine vinegar
1 shallot, finely minced
1 teaspoon freshly cracked black peppercorns
½ cup white vinegar
¼ Granny Smith apple, peeled and cored
¼ loosely packed cup cilantro leaves
1 small garlic clove
Cocktail sauce

Spread out the sea salt on two plates and arrange the oyster shells in the salt so the oysters do not tip and spill their "liquor." Refrigerate.

Mix together the red wine vinegar, shallots, and pepper. Set aside.

Combine the white vinegar, apple, cilantro, and garlic in a blender and purée until smooth.

To serve, arrange 12 oysters on each serving plate. Drizzle the red vinegar sauce over 4 of the oysters on each plate. Place a small dollop of the cilantro-apple sauce on 4 of the oysters on each plate, and spoon cocktail sauce on the remaining 4 oysters on each plate. Serve cold with champagne or a crisp white wine.

Fruit Bat Pizza Bites

Serves 6

1 pound sugar cookie dough
8 ounces cream cheese, softened
½ cup powdered sugar
6 sliced strawberries
½ mango, cut in slices
1 sliced banana
¼ cup blueberries
¼ cup apple jelly

Preheat oven to 350°F. Press the sugar cookie dough out onto a 12" pizza pan.

Bake the cookie dough for 20 minutes, then let cool on a rack.

Whip the cream cheese. Add the powdered sugar and mix well.

Spread the cookie dough with the cream cheese mixture.

Arrange the fruit on top of the cream cheese, glaze the fruit with warm apple jelly, and chill for 10 minutes. Cut into wedges to serve.

Serves 4–6

4 ounces Manchego cheese
4 ounces Cabrales blue cheese
4 ounces Tetilla cheese
4 ounces of Jamón Serrano (cured Spanish ham)
4 pinquillo red peppers
½ cup manzanilla olives
¼ cup Marcona almonds
2 ounces membrillo (quince paste)
1 loaf of crusty bread, sliced

Slice the Manchego, Cabrales, and Tetilla cheeses and place them on a platter.

Slice the Jamón Serrano and place on the platter.

Arrange the peppers, olives, almonds, and quince paste on the platter.

Place the bread in a basket and serve with the cheese plate.

Serves 4–6

3 ounces Parmigiano-Reggiano cheese
3 ounces ricotta salata cheese
3 ounces Gorgonzola blue cheese
3 ounces Fontina cheese
8 mozzarella boconcini cheeses

Crumble the Parmigiano-Reggiano and place it on a platter.

Put the ricotta salata, Gorgonzola, and Fontina on the platter in their whole pieces. Arrange the mozzarella boconcini around the other cheeses.

Serve with a knife and serving fork.

TASTY TIDBIT

IF YOU'RE OF ITALIAN ANCESTRY OR JUST A FAN OF SPAGHETTI BOLOGNESE, THEN IT'S LIKELY YOU HAVE GARLIC IN YOUR KITCHEN—NICE FAT BULBS OF THE STINKING ROSE! GARLIC IS ONE OF THE MOST COMMONLY THOUGHT OF ITEMS USED TO WARD OFF VAMPIRES, AND A IT'S A PROTECTION DEVICE AGAINST EVIL THAT'S EXISTED SINCE ANCIENT TIMES. GIVEN THAT A VAMPIRE'S SENSES ARE HEIGHTENED, PARTICULARLY ITS VISION, HEARING, AND SMELL, IT STANDS TO REASON THAT GARLIC, WHETHER IT'S WORN AROUND THE NECK AS A WREATH, STREWN AROUND A HOUSE, OR EVEN LIQUEFIED AND SPRAYED WOULD BE ENOUGH TO KEEP THE UNDEAD AT BAY.

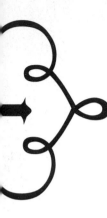

Trampy Scampi Bites

Serves 6

3 boneless, skinless chicken breasts
½ cup panko breadcrumbs
2 tablespoons chopped fresh parsley
½ cup Parmesan cheese
1 egg, beaten
2 ounces salted butter
1 minced garlic clove
¼ cup lemon juice

Preheat oven to 375°F.

Cut the chicken into uniform bite-sized pieces.

Combine the breadcrumbs, parsley, and Parmesan cheese in a bowl.

Dip the chicken pieces in the egg, then coat with breadcrumb mixture. Place the chicken pieces in a 9" × 13" glass baking dish.

Melt the butter, garlic, and lemon juice in a skillet. Gently pour half of this mixture over the chicken pieces. Bake uncovered for 45 minutes. Spoon the rest of the lemon garlic butter over the chicken and serve hot.

Love at First Bite

Sicilian Blood Red Gravy Fondue

Serves 6

¼ cup olive oil
1 onion, chopped
3 cloves garlic, minced
1 green bell pepper, diced
1 teaspoon dried oregano
1 teaspoon dried basil
6 ounces tomato paste
1 cup red wine

1½ quarts water
1 (32-ounce) can diced tomatoes
1 (16-ounce) can tomato sauce
1 teaspoon hot pepper flakes
¼ cup fresh parsley, finely chopped
Salt and pepper to taste
Parsley to taste
1 tablespoon sugar

In a large, heavy saucepan or Dutch oven, heat the olive oil over medium-high heat. Add onion, garlic, and bell pepper. Cook, stirring, until onion turns translucent, about 5 minutes. Add oregano and basil. Stir well.

Stir tomato paste into the oil for 1 minute. Add 1 cup of red wine and mix until blended. Add tomatoes, tomato sauce, and pepper flakes. Pour 1½ quarts of water into the sauce and reduce heat to medium.

Simmer sauce for 2 hours, stirring occasionally and adding water if sauce becomes too thick. When sauce reaches desired consistency, season with salt, pepper, and parsley. Stir in sugar and bring to a boil.

Remove sauce from heat and ladle into 1 or more fondue pots. Place pot over heating source. Serve with meatballs, shrimp, and sausage.

Punish Me Pizza Bites

10 mini pizzas

1 can refrigerated biscuits
¾ cup pasta sauce
¾ cup shredded mozzarella cheese

Preheat the oven to 375°F.

Open biscuit can and separate biscuits.

Flatten out each of the biscuits onto a cookie sheet.

Using a large spoon, spread about 1 tablespoon of the pasta sauce over each biscuit. Top with about 1 tablespoon of the mozzarella cheese.

Bake pizzas for 8 to 10 minutes, or until crusts are golden brown and cheese is melted.

Jaw-Snapping Sausage Bites
5–6 dozen

2 pounds bulk pork sausage
2 eggs, slightly beaten
1 cup fine dry bread crumbs, plain
½ cup milk
1 teaspoon ground sage
½ teaspoon leaf thyme, crumbled
1 cup water
⅔ cup ketchup
¼ cup brown sugar, packed
2 tablespoons vinegar
2 tablespoons soy sauce

In a large bowl, combine the sausage, beaten eggs, bread crumbs, milk, sage, and thyme. With an electric mixer or food processor, beat until well blended.

With wet hands, shape mixture into balls about 1" to 1¼" in diameter.

In a large skillet, arrange a batch of sausage balls in a single layer; brown on all sides. This will take about 12 to 15 minutes for each batch. When all sausage bites are browned, pour off excess fat and return to the skillet, or transfer to a large sauce-pan or Dutch oven.

Combine remaining ingredients; pour over sausage. Cover and simmer for 15 minutes, stirring occasionally.

Serve hot from slow cooker or chafing dish, with toothpicks for spearing the sausage bites.

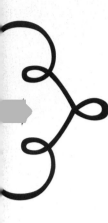

Love Bites

Serves 4

⅓ cup honey
2 teaspoons fresh ginger, minced
2 teaspoons lemon juice
2 teaspoons cider vinegar
2 teaspoons low-sodium soy sauce
½ teaspoon dark sesame oil
½ teaspoon freshly squeezed orange juice
⅓ teaspoon Worcestershire sauce
1 clove fresh garlic, minced
½ pound boneless, skinless chicken breast, cut in 1" cubes
½ teaspoon salt
1 teaspoon cornstarch
1 teaspoon water

Combine all ingredients in a container with a lid and mix well. Cover the chicken and let marinate for at least 1 hour.

Coat a cookie sheet with nonstick spray. Remove chicken from marinade and place on cookie sheet without crowding.

Bake at 425°F for 15 to 20 minutes, turning once.

Love at First Bite

CHAPTER 2

SUCKULENT SOUPS AND STEWS

Suppers and Snacks
to Sip and Slurp

Bloody Beef Stew

Serves 2

1 tablespoon vegetable oil
2 baby onions, cut in half
4 ounces sliced fresh mushrooms
1 zucchini, thinly sliced
¼ teaspoon dried oregano
2 cups leftover cooked beef, cubed
¼ cup burgundy
½ cup beef broth
1 tablespoon tomato paste
1 tablespoon Worcestershire sauce
⅛ teaspoon black pepper

Heat the oil in a skillet on medium heat. Add the onions, mushrooms, and zucchini. Stir in the dried oregano. Sauté for about 5 minutes, until the vegetables are softened.

Add the beef. Cook for 2 to 3 minutes to heat through.

Add the burgundy and beef broth. Stir in the tomato paste and Worcestershire sauce. Bring to a boil.

Stir in the pepper. Turn down the heat and simmer for about 5 minutes. Serve hot.

Love at First Bite

Blood-Chilling Gazpacho

Serves 8

6 large ripe tomatoes, chopped
1 small red onion, chopped
1 cucumber, peeled and chopped
1 green pepper, seeded and chopped
2 cloves garlic, peeled and chopped
1 stalk celery, chopped
¼ cup fresh parsley
¼ cup red wine vinegar
¼ cup extra-virgin olive oil
1 teaspoon Worcestershire sauce
1 teaspoon sugar
3 cups tomato juice
1 large avocado, finely diced

Combine all ingredients except tomato juice and avocado in a blender or food processor. Pulse until puréed.

Strain mixture through a coarse sieve into a glass bowl or pitcher. Press to extract all the juices. Stir in the tomato juice, cover, and refrigerate until well-chilled.

Just before serving, dice avocado. Pour gazpacho into soup cups and garnish with diced avocado.

Cold-Blooded Avocado Soup

Serves 6

1 medium yellow onion
2 ripe avocados
4 cups chicken broth
1 medium canned tomatillo
1/2 cup fresh cilantro leaves
1/4 cup canned jalapeño peppers
3/4 teaspoon garlic paste
1 teaspoon salt
1/2 teaspoon ground red pepper
1 cup sour cream
1/4 cup lime juice

Remove skin from onion and quarter. Remove skin and pits from avocados then cut into 2" pieces. Combine all ingredients except sour cream and lime juice in a food processor or blender. You may need to do 2 or 3 batches. Blend on medium setting until ingredients are well melded and smooth.

Refrigerate for 3 hours. Remove any fat that has congealed on the top of the soup. Stir and refrigerate for an additional hour. Top with a dollop of sour cream and a sprinkle of lime juice before serving.

Love at First Bite

Lovers Chili

Serves 2

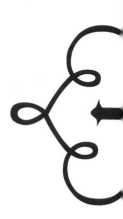

½ large white or yellow onion
2 tablespoons vegetable oil
1 (15-ounce) can red kidney beans
1 (8½-ounce) can corn
1 medium-size zucchini (about 8" long)
1 (14½-ounce) can stewed tomatoes, with juice
1 tablespoon chili powder
2 teaspoons oregano

Chop the onion. In a frying pan, cook the onion in the vegetable oil over medium-high heat, stirring constantly until tender. Transfer the onion and oil to a Dutch oven, stew pot, or 2-quart slow cooker.

Drain the kidney beans and corn. Add to the pot.

Rinse the zucchini under cold, running water. Chop the zucchini and add to the pot.

Stir in the tomatoes with their juice. Add the chili powder and oregano. In a Dutch oven or stew pot, cover and bring to a boil over medium-high heat. Reduce heat to low. Cook for about 15 minutes, until the zucchini is tender. Uncover for the last 5 minutes. In a slow cooker, cover and cook for 1 hour on high. Reduce heat to low until ready to serve. Uncover for the last 5 minutes.

Crimson Gazpacho

Serves 6

1 clove garlic
5 ripe tomatoes
3 cucumbers
1 green bell pepper
½ cup minced onion
3 cups tomato juice
¼ cup extra-virgin olive oil
3 tablespoons lemon juice
1 teaspoon salt
⅛ teaspoon pepper
2 tablespoons chopped parsley

Cut the garlic in half and rub the serving bowl with garlic; discard garlic. Chop the tomatoes and place half into food processor or blender. Peel cucumber, remove seeds with a spoon, and chop; place half in food processor. Process the tomatoes and cucumbers until smooth; pour into bowl.

Chop the green bell pepper and add to serving bowl along with remaining chopped tomatoes, cucumber, and onion. Slowly stir in remaining ingredients. Cover and chill for 2 to 3 hours before serving.

Love at First Bite

Miso Thirsty Soup
Serves 4

3 cups water
4 tablespoons miso
½ cup cubed tofu
1 sliced green onion

Boil the water and combine it with the miso.

Divide the tofu among four bowls. Pour the miso broth into the bowls and garnish with the green onion.

Serve hot.

TASTY TIDBIT

IN SOME LEGENDS, STAKES WERE POUNDED INTO THE GROUND ABOVE A GRAVE TO ENSURE THAT A REANIMATED CORPSE WOULD BE STAKED IF HE ATTEMPTED TO ARISE FROM THE EARTH. IN OTHERS, THE CORPSES' HEADS WERE STAKED TO SECURE THEM TO THE GROUND. A FEW LEGENDS CALL FOR A CORPSE TO BE STAKED THROUGH THE BACK AND BURIED FACE DOWN TO PREVENT HIM DIGGING HIS WAY UP AND OUT. IN ADDITION TO STAKING, SOME CORPSES WERE ALSO BEHEADED, THEIR MOUTHS STUFFED WITH GARLIC, OR THEIR HEARTS REMOVED AND BURNED TO CINDERS.

Killer Chili

Serves 6–8

2 cups dried pinto beans, soaked overnight
3 pounds ground venison
2 onions, chopped
3 cloves garlic, minced
1 (28-ounce) can fire-roasted tomatoes
2 tablespoons cider vinegar
1 chipotle pepper from a can of chipotle peppers in adobo sauce
1 teaspoon adobo sauce
3 tablespoons chili powder
1 tablespoon ground cumin
Kosher salt and freshly ground black pepper to taste
2 cups sharp Cheddar cheese, shredded
1 red onion, diced
1 cup mixed fresh herbs, chopped (parsley, cilantro, and chives)

After soaking overnight, rinse pinto beans well and set aside.

Brown meat in a large pot over medium-high heat. Add onions and garlic and cook until soft, about 7 to 8 minutes. Add can of tomatoes and cider vinegar.

Finely chop the chipotle pepper and add to the pot. Add adobo sauce, chili powder, and cumin and season with salt and pepper to taste. Stir well and bring to a boil.

Add 2 or 3 cups of water if chili is too thick; readjust seasonings. Turn heat down to a simmer and cover. Cook for 30 minutes or longer.

Set cheese, red onion, and herbs in separate bowls for garnishing. Then serve chili.

Love at First Bite

Vlad's Vichyssoise

Serves 4

3 potatoes, peeled and diced
1 leek (white part only), diced
2 cups water
1 cup heavy cream
Salt and pepper to taste
Chopped chives

Boil potatoes and leeks in water until tender, about 25 minutes.

Purée leek, potato, and water mixture in blender; add cream, salt, and pepper, and blend well.

Chill thoroughly before serving. To serve, thin out with more cream if necessary and garnish with chopped chives.

TASTY TIDBIT

VLAD THE IMPALER WAS THE FOURTEENTH-CENTURY RULER OF WALLACHIA WHO BECAME INFAMOUS FOR IMPALING HIS ENEMIES ON POLES AND FAMOUS IN ROMANIA AS A NATIONAL HERO. VLAD DRACULA WAS THE INSPIRATION FOR THE NAME OF BRAM STOKER'S TITLE CHARACTER IN THE NOVEL *DRACULA*.

Hobo Stew

Serves 4

1 pound ground beef
¾ cup dry bread crumbs
2 tablespoons Worcestershire sauce
1 tablespoon ketchup
1 tablespoon Dijon mustard
1 teaspoon onion powder
¼ cup Parmesan cheese
1 egg, beaten
½ teaspoon salt
½ teaspoon pepper
1 cup peeled potatoes, large pieces
½ cup sliced onion
½ cup sliced carrot

Preheat oven to 350°F. Tear off 4 large squares of heavy-duty aluminum foil. Set aside.

In a bowl, combine the ground beef, bread crumbs, Worcestershire sauce, ketchup, mustard, onion powder, cheese, egg, salt, and pepper with your hands. Form the meat mixture into 4 oblong patties.

Set one patty on each foil square. Divide potatoes, onions, and carrots into four servings. Place one serving on top of each meat patty. Sprinkle the vegetables with salt and pepper.

Wrap each foil square up around the meat and vegetables into a tightly sealed packet.

Place the packets on a baking sheet. Bake for 45 minutes. Remove packets from the oven and carefully open them, avoiding the steam that will be released.

Love at First Bite

Foul Fowl Soup

Serves 4

4 ounces skinless, boneless chicken breast
1 tablespoon water
2 teaspoons Chinese rice wine or dry sherry
4 cups chicken stock or broth
1/4 teaspoon salt
1/8 teaspoon white pepper
1 can creamed corn
1 tablespoon cornstarch mixed with 4 tablespoons water
2 egg whites, lightly beaten
2 green onions, sliced

Cut the chicken into chunks and place in a food processor. Add the water and 1 teaspoon rice wine, and mince the chicken into a fine paste.

Bring the broth or stock to a boil. Add the salt, white pepper, 1 teaspoon rice wine, and creamed corn. Add the chicken paste, stirring so that the chicken breaks up into small pieces. Cook until the chicken turns white.

Mix the cornstarch and water, and pour the mixture into the soup, stirring to thicken. Turn off the heat.

Pour the eggs into the soup in a steady stream, and quickly stir in a clockwise direction until they form thin shreds.

Add the green onions and give the soup a final stir.

Serves 6

8 cups water
2 cups dried split peas
1 ham bone
½ cup diced carrots
¼ cup diced celery
1 cup diced onions
Salt to taste
Pepper to taste

Simmer water, split peas, and ham bone for 1 hour.

Add carrots, celery, and onions and simmer for 1 hour more.

Remove ham bone and season with salt and pepper.

Serves 6

1 tablespoon olive oil

1 onion, chopped

2 cloves garlic, minced

2 stalks celery, chopped

1 tablespoon curry powder

2 teaspoons sugar

¼ teaspoon salt

⅛ teaspoon pepper

1 (16-ounce) package frozen
baby peas

2 cups vegetable broth

2 cups water

1 cup nonfat light cream

2 tablespoons lemon juice

½ cup low-fat sour cream

½ cup grated cucumber, drained

¼ cup chopped green onions

Pinch grated nutmeg

In large soup pot, heat olive oil over medium heat. Add onion and garlic; cook and stir for 4 minutes. Add celery and curry powder; cook and stir for 4 to 5 minutes longer until tender.

Add sugar, salt, pepper, and peas; cook and stir for 2 minutes. Add broth and water; bring to a simmer. Reduce heat to low, cover pot, and simmer for 6 to 7 minutes until everything is tender.

Remove from heat and stir in light cream and lemon juice. Using an immersion blender, purée the soup. Pour into a large bowl, cover by placing plastic wrap directly on the soup, and refrigerate until cold, about 3 to 4 hours.

When ready to serve, combine sour cream, cucumber, green onion, and nutmeg in small bowl. Serve the soup in chilled bowls and top with sour cream mixture.

Count Orlock's Cucumber Soup

Serves 6

1 cup sliced yellow onion
3 cups fish stock (or clam stock)
3 cups peeled, seeded, and diced cucumber (about ½" pieces)
2 tablespoons chopped dill
2½ cups plain yogurt
Salt, to taste
Freshly cracked black pepper, to taste

Combine the onions, fish stock, and cucumbers in a medium-sized saucepan and bring to a simmer over low heat. Cook for about 5 minutes, until the cucumbers are tender but not mushy. Transfer the mixture to a food processor fitted with a metal blade and process until smooth. Add the dill and yogurt, and pulse until just combined. Season with salt and pepper and transfer to a bowl. Refrigerate until chilled. (The soup can be made ahead up to this point.)

To serve, ladle the soup into chilled bowls.

TASTY TIDBIT

COUNT ORLOCK IS THE HIDEOUS, RAT-FACED DRACULA PLAYED BY GERMAN ACTOR MAX SCHRECK IN THE 1922 FILM *NOSFERATU*. (FOR AN ADDED DOSE OF IRONY, THE WORD *SCHRECK* IS GERMAN FOR "FRIGHT.")

Deathly Cold Zucchini Squash Soup

Serves 6

3 tablespoons olive oil
½ cup finely chopped leeks (white and light green parts only)
4 cups thinly sliced zucchini squash
4 cups chicken stock
1 tablespoon fresh-squeezed lemon juice
½ cup half-and-half
½ cup sour cream
2 tablespoons finely chopped fresh chives
6 tablespoons finely chopped fresh basil
Salt, to taste
Freshly ground black pepper, to taste

Heat the oil in a large saucepan over medium heat and sauté the leeks until softened, about 5 to 7 minutes. Add the squash and sauté for another 5 minutes, or until lightly browned.

Add the stock, cover, and cook for about 15 minutes, until the squash is tender. Use a slotted spoon to transfer the zucchini to a food processor fitted with a metal blade or to a blender; process to a smooth purée, adding a few tablespoons of the hot stock if necessary. Transfer the soup to a bowl and refrigerate. (The soup may be made ahead up to this point.)

After the soup has been chilled, add the lemon juice, half-and-half, sour cream, chives, and 3 tablespoons of the basil. Season with salt and pepper. Taste and adjust seasoning as desired.

Serve in chilled soup bowls, garnished with the remaining 3 tablespoons basil.

Masochistic Lion's Head Meatball Stew
Serves 2–4

1 pound ground pork
1 tablespoon soy sauce
1 teaspoon sugar
½ teaspoon sesame oil
2 tablespoons Chinese rice wine or dry sherry
2 bunches spinach leaves
3 tablespoons oil for stir-frying
1 cup chicken broth or stock
¼ teaspoon salt

Place the pork in a medium-sized bowl. Mix in the soy sauce, sugar, sesame oil, and 1 tablespoon rice wine. Marinate for 20 minutes.

Wash the spinach leaves. Blanch the spinach in boiling water briefly, just until the leaves begin to wilt. Drain thoroughly.

Form the marinated pork into 4 large meatballs, each roughly the size of a tennis ball. (Alternately, you can make the meatballs the size of golf balls, which will give you more meatballs.)

Add oil to a preheated wok or skillet. Fry the meatballs on medium heat for 5 minutes on each side, until they brown. (The meatballs will not be cooked through.) Remove and drain on paper towels.

While the meatballs are frying, preheat the oven to 375°F.

Bring the chicken broth or stock to a boil. Stir in the salt and 1 tablespoon rice wine. Remove from the heat.

Line the bottom of a casserole dish with the spinach leaves. Add the meatballs and pour the chicken stock mixture over. Bake at 375°F for 30 minutes, or until the meatballs are cooked through.

Love at First Bite

Blood Bowl

Serves 8

2 pounds beef sirloin tips
¼ cup flour
1 teaspoon ground red chili powder
2 tablespoons lard or bacon grease
2 onions, chopped
4 cloves garlic, minced
3 dried ancho peppers
3 cups water
3 (14-ounce) cans beef broth
2 jalapeño peppers, minced
2 teaspoons chili paste
1 teaspoon cumin
3 tablespoons chili powder
½ teaspoon dried oregano
1½ teaspoons salt
½ teaspoon pepper

Cut beef into 1" pieces if necessary and toss with flour and red chili powder. Melt lard or bacon grease in large stockpot over medium heat. Sauté coated beef in batches until brown, about 4 to 5 minutes per batch. Remove each batch when cooked. Cook onions and garlic in drippings until crisp-tender, about 4 to 5 minutes.

Meanwhile, soak ancho peppers in ½ cup hot water for about 30 minutes. Drain and purée peppers and ¼ cup water in blender or food processor. Add to onions in pot along with beef and remaining ingredients. Bring to a boil, then cover pot, reduce heat to low, and simmer for 2½ hours, stirring occasionally.

The Celery Stalks at Midnight Soup

Serves 6

4 cups chicken broth
6 stalks celery with leaves, chopped
½ cup baby peas
1 teaspoon Splenda
Salt and pepper to taste
1 tablespoon lemon juice
¼ cup celeriac, peeled and julienned
Fresh parsley and chives, chopped, for garnish

Place all ingredients except celeriac and the garnish in a blender.

Purée until smooth.

Serve in chilled cups with celeriac, parsley, and chives floated on top.

Demon Ghoulash

Serves 4–6

2½ pounds lamb
2 onions
2½ pounds potatoes
Salt and pepper
4–6 cups chicken broth
2 tablespoons chopped parsley (optional)

Preheat the oven to 375°F. Trim off excess fat and cut the lamb into pieces, through the bones. Thinly slice the onions and potatoes.

Place these 3 ingredients in layers in an oven-ready casserole dish, sprinkling each layer with salt and pepper. A layer of potatoes should be on top.

Pour in enough broth to fill the casserole halfway up. Cover. Bake for 2 hours. Uncover and bake for an additional 30 minutes. Sprinkle with parsley and serve.

Serves 6

1½ pounds sirloin tip, cubed
2 onions, chopped
4 cloves garlic, minced
4 carrots, sliced
½ teaspoon salt
½ teaspoon dried thyme leaves
⅛ teaspoon pepper
4 cups low-sodium beef stock
3 cups water
1 cup low-fat sour cream
2 tablespoons flour
2 cups whole wheat egg noodles
¼ cup chopped chives

In 4-quart slow cooker, combine beef, onions, garlic, carrots, salt, thyme, pepper, beef stock, and water. Cover and cook on low for 7 to 8 hours or until beef and vegetables are tender.

In small bowl combine sour cream with flour. Add 1 cup of the hot liquid from slow cooker; mix with wire whisk. Add sour cream mixture to slow cooker. Cover and cook on high for 20 to 25 minutes or until soup thickens. Stir in egg noodles; cook for 6 to 7 minutes longer until noodles are tender.

Serve immediately, topped with chives.

Serves 8

2 tablespoons olive oil
1 pound lean round or chuck, diced
1 large onion, diced
1 rib celery, sliced
1 green bell pepper, cored and diced
1 beet, peeled and diced
1 large potato, peeled and diced
2 (16-ounce) cans diced tomatoes
8 cups beef broth
1 teaspoon caraway seed
1 small cabbage, cored and diced
1 tablespoon lemon juice
Salt and pepper to taste

In a large, heavy soup pan, heat oil over medium-high heat. Brown beef cubes; remove to a plate. Add onion, celery, and green pepper; sauté over medium-high heat 3 minutes.

Add beet, potato, tomatoes, and broth. Return beef to pot; bring to a boil.

Reduce heat to medium; add caraway; simmer 30 minutes.

Add cabbage; continue cooking 1½ hours.

Stir in lemon juice, salt, and pepper. Remove from heat; let stand briefly before serving.

Transylvanian Turkey Chowder

Serves 10

2 stalks celery
1 onion
1 green bell pepper
3 carrots
3 russet potatoes
2 tablespoons butter
2 cups chicken or giblet broth
3 cups cooked turkey, cubed
1 cup corn kernels
3 cups milk
¾ teaspoon thyme
Salt and pepper
Fresh chopped parsley (optional)

Thinly slice the celery and onion, chop the bell pepper, slice the carrots, and dice the potatoes.

In a soup pot, heat the butter on medium heat. Add the onion and green pepper, sautéing for 4 minutes. Add the broth and the carrots, bring to a boil, reduce to a simmer, and cook for 5 more minutes.

Add the potatoes and celery, simmering the mixture for an additional 10 minutes.

Stir in the turkey, corn kernels, milk, and thyme; salt and pepper to taste. Heat gently, but thoroughly. Garnish with parsley and serve.

MINA-strone Soup with Meatballs

Serves 6

24 cooked meatballs
1 (15-ounce) can navy or other white beans, drained
1 tablespoon dried minced onion
1 teaspoon basil
1 bay leaf
2 cups beef broth
2 cups water
1 cup ditali, orzo, or other pasta
1 (16-ounce) can diced tomatoes (liquid retained)
1 (10-ounce) package frozen mixed vegetables, thawed
Parmesan cheese, grated

In a 4-quart saucepan, combine the meatballs, beans, onion, basil, bay leaf, broth, and water; bring to a boil.

Add the pasta and cook for 15 minutes.

Reduce to a simmer and add the tomatoes with liquid and the vegetables; heat through. Serve in individual bowls, topped with grated Parmesan cheese.

TASTY TIDBIT

Mina Murray—Dracula's obsession—is actively involved in the hunt for him and is second only to Van Helsing in her knowledge and strategy. In *The League of Extraordinary Gentlemen* comic, she wears a scarf all the time, because her throat was nearly torn out by Dracula.

Putrid Pumpkin Soup

Serves 6–8

1 small pumpkin (2½–3 pounds)
1 onion (yellow or red)
2 tablespoons olive oil or butter
½ teaspoon cinnamon
½ teaspoon ground cumin
¼ teaspoon curry powder
5 cups vegetable or chicken broth
¼ cup orange juice
2 teaspoons grated fresh ginger (optional)

Cut the pumpkin in half and scrape out the seeds and slimy threads. (Wash and save the seeds for later use, if you like.) Cut the pumpkin into chunks (this makes it easier to peel) and remove the peel. Cut the flesh into small chunks. Chop the onion.

In a soup pot, warm the oil. Add the onion and sauté on medium for 3 minutes. Add the pumpkin, along with the spices; cook briefly, stirring, until well mixed. Pour in the broth and the orange juice. Bring to a boil, reduce to simmer, and cook for 30 to 40 minutes.

Remove from heat and let cool slightly. Using a blender or food processor, purée the mixture. Return it to soup pot to rewarm, adding a bit more orange juice or a little milk to achieve the desired thickness. Garnish with the fresh ginger, if using.

Love at First Bite

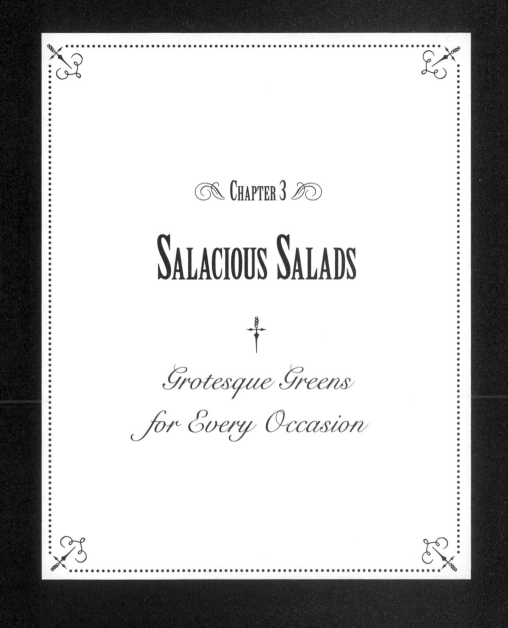

Chapter 3

Salacious Salads

Grotesque Greens
for Every Occasion

Chopped to Bits Salad

Serves 8

5 cups iceberg and romaine lettuce, chopped
1 cup red cabbage, chopped
1 cup carrots, finely diced
1 cup radishes (unpeeled), finely diced
1 cup celery, finely diced
1 cup cauliflower, finely chopped
½ cup red bell pepper, finely diced
½ cup yellow summer squash, finely diced
1 cup green peas or edamame, cooked and chilled
⅓ cup red onion, minced
1 cup extra-virgin olive oil
⅓ cup red wine vinegar
1 teaspoon Dijon mustard
1 clove garlic, minced
1 teaspoon soy sauce
2 tablespoons sugar

In a large glass salad bowl, place chopped lettuces. Spread cabbage over lettuces in a single layer.

In a separate bowl, combine carrots, radishes, celery, cauliflower, bell pepper, squash, peas or edamame, and red onion.

Whisk together olive oil, vinegar, mustard, garlic, soy, and sugar. Pour over chopped vegetables and mix well.

Spoon chopped vegetables over lettuces in salad bowl and serve.

Love at First Bite

Corpulent Crudité

Serves 4

1 green bell pepper
1 carrot
2 stalks celery
1 cucumber
1 medium-sized red onion
1 teaspoon lemon juice
3 tablespoons vegetable oil
½ teaspoon water
¼ teaspoon basil
¼ teaspoon salt

Rinse the green bell pepper, carrot, celery, and cucumber in cold, running water. Peel the carrot and cucumber. Chop all the vegetables and place in a large mixing bowl. Chop the onion and add it to the bowl.

In a small mixing bowl, stir together the lemon juice, vegetable oil, water, basil, and salt until well mixed. Pour the mixture over the chopped vegetables. Stir until the vegetables are well coated. Cover and refrigerate at least 1 hour until ready to serve.

Moroccan Blood Orange and Red Onion Salad
Serves 4

3 blood oranges
1 small red onion, peeled
2 tablespoons olive oil
2 teaspoons lemon juice
Salt and pepper to taste
1 tablespoon chopped fresh parsley

Cut the top and bottom off the oranges and stand them up on their cut ends. With a serrated paring knife, cut away the rind in top-to-bottom strips. Remove as much white pith as you can.

Turn the oranges on their sides and cut crosswise into slices. Arrange the orange slices on a plate.

Cut slices from the onion crosswise and scatter them across the orange slices.

Put the olive oil, lemon juice, salt, pepper, and parsley in a jar with a lid and shake the ingredients together.

Pour the vinaigrette over the oranges and onions and serve at room temperature or chilled.

Love at First Bite

Slaw to Slay Them All

Serves 4

½ pound celery root
¼ cup minced shallots
¼ cup olive oil
2 tablespoons lemon juice
1 teaspoon grated lemon zest
1 teaspoon Dijon mustard
Salt and pepper to taste
2 tablespoons chopped chives

Peel the celery root and cut it into ¼"-thick slices. Stack the slices a few at a time and cut them into julienne strips. Place the strips in a large bowl.

Put the shallots, olive oil, lemon juice, lemon zest, mustard, salt, pepper, and chives in a jar with a lid and shake to combine.

Pour the dressing over the celery root and toss to combine. Cover and refrigerate for at least 1 hour.

Sanguinarian Salad

Serves 4

1 pint fresh strawberries, sliced
½ cup sugar
1 tablespoon poppy seeds
2 teaspoons minced onion
¼ teaspoon Worcestershire sauce
¼ teaspoon paprika
¼ cup cider vinegar
½ cup canola oil
salt and pepper to taste
2 bunches baby spinach leaves
¼ red onion, sliced

Purée ¼ of the strawberries in a blender.

Add sugar, poppy seeds, minced onion, Worcestershire sauce, paprika, and vinegar to the blender. Mix well.

Add oil in a stream with the blender running. Season dressing with salt and pepper.

Toss spinach, remaining strawberries, and red onion with the dressing.

Serve with freshly ground black pepper.

TASTY TIDBIT

A SANGUINARIAN IS A PERSON WHO HAS A HOBBY OF DRINK-ING BLOOD, EVEN IF THEY ARE NOT IMMORTAL.

Lost Boys Lobster Salad
Serves 2

2 cups arugula or baby mixed salad greens
1 cooked and shelled lobster, chilled
¼ cup vinaigrette (below)
½ cup cherry tomatoes, cut in half
½ cup mayonnaise
5 chopped fresh basil leaves

Toss greens and lobster meat with vinaigrette (see recipe below), divide evenly, and arrange on plates.

Scatter cherry tomatoes around greens.

Mix together mayonnaise and basil. Spoon mayonnaise mixture onto plates for dipping.

Virulent Vinaigrette
Serves 8

½ teaspoon Dijon mustard
1 tablespoon minced shallots
¼ cup red wine vinegar
1 cup olive oil
Salt and pepper to taste

Combine mustard, shallots, and vinegar in a bowl with a whisk.

Drizzle in olive oil while whisking, and season with salt and pepper.

Store in a jar and shake to combine before using.

Serves 4

½ cup diced onion
¼ cup diced carrot
¼ cup diced celery
4 tablespoons olive oil
1 cup wild rice
2½ cups low-sodium chicken broth
½ teaspoon chopped fresh thyme
1 teaspoon salt
¼ teaspoon pepper

In a large sauté pan, sauté the onion, carrot, and celery in the olive oil until tender.

Add the wild rice to the sautéed vegetables and stir over medium heat for a few minutes. This scratches the outer husk of the rice so that the liquid can be absorbed more easily.

Pour the rice and vegetables into a baking dish.

Add the broth, thyme, salt, and pepper; stir to incorporate.

Cover and bake for 45 minutes to 1 hour.

Serves 4

2 cups cooked wild rice, warm
¼ cup diced red bell pepper
¼ cup diced sun-dried tomatoes
½ cup chopped pecans
2 tablespoons balsamic vinegar
Salt and pepper to taste

Mix everything together while the wild rice is still warm, so that the rice can absorb the most flavor.

Chill mixture.

Adjust seasoning. Serve cold.

TASTY TIDBIT

ARGUABLY THE MOST EVIL TWIST TO THE DESTRUCTIVE CAPABILITIES OF SUNLIGHT IS THE FACT THAT VAMPIRES OFTEN USE IT TO KILL OTHER VAMPIRES. IN *INTERVIEW WITH THE VAMPIRE*, ANNE RICE MAKES USE OF THIS, ASSIGNING THE FATE TO CLAUDIA AND GABRIELLE FOR ATTEMPTING TO KILL LESTAT. IN THE FILM *UNDERWORLD*, VAMPIRE ELDER VIKTOR BESTOWED THE SAME FATE ON HIS DAUGHTER SONJA FOR CARRYING A CHILD CONCEIVED WITH LYCAN LEADER, LUCIAN.

Transylvanian Treats
Serves 6

2 cucumbers, seedless variety
4 strips bacon
½ cup finely chopped romaine lettuce
⅛ cup finely diced tomato, flesh only, no seeds
⅛ cup shredded Cheddar cheese
¼ cup mayonnaise
¼ teaspoon salt
Freshly cracked black pepper, to taste

Rinse cucumber and pat dry. Trim off about 1" from each end. Peel the cucumbers entirely or "stripe" them by leaving alternating strips of peel.

Prepare 12 cucumber cups by cutting the cucumbers into slices about 1" to 1¼" thick; use a melon baller to scoop out the center of each slice, about ¾" deep. Place the cups upside down on paper towels and set aside.

Cook the bacon until crispy (either in the microwave or on the stovetop).

Dice the cooked bacon and transfer to a medium-sized bowl. Add the lettuce, tomatoes, Cheddar, mayonnaise, salt, and pepper; lightly blend with a fork until evenly mixed. The mixture should be tossed until just combined, not mashed down with the fork.

To assemble, arrange the cups on a serving platter. Use a teaspoon to fill each cup with the bacon mixture until nicely mounded on the top and serve.

Love at First Bite

Frightful Filet Mignon Caesar Salad
Serves 2

2 (6-ounce) filet mignons, each wrapped in a strip of bacon
½ teaspoon kosher salt
½ teaspoon freshly ground black pepper
2 cups roughly chopped hearts of romaine
¼ cup prepared Caesar dressing
2 tablespoons freshly grated Parmesan cheese
6 anchovy fillets, drained and rolled into pinwheels

Pat the steaks dry with paper towels. Lightly season the steaks with salt and pepper. Heat an indoor grill pan or a sauté pan over medium-high heat. Cook the steaks to desired doneness, 4 to 6 minutes per side for medium-rare. Transfer the filets to a plate and tent with tinfoil to keep warm.

Toss together the lettuce, half of the dressing, and the Parmesan cheese. Add additional dressing to achieve desired consistency. To serve, divide the salad between 2 dinner plates. Add a hot filet and 3 of the anchovies to each plate.

Deviled Egg Salad

Serves 3

6 hard-boiled eggs, peeled
2 tablespoons Dijon mustard
¼ teaspoon seasoned salt
½ teaspoon paprika
Freshly cracked black pepper, to taste
2 tablespoons chili sauce
1–2 tablespoons mayonnaise

Cut the eggs in half lengthwise and remove the yolks. Set aside the whites. Place the yolks in a small bowl and add the mustard, salt, paprika, pepper, and chili sauce. Use a fork to blend into a paste-like consistency. Add the mayonnaise, teaspoon by teaspoon, until a somewhat creamy consistency is achieved.

Finely chop the reserved egg whites and season with salt and pepper. Use a rubber spatula to fold the whites into the yolk mixture. Refrigerate until ready to serve. Garnish with additional paprika if desired.

Divinity Salad
Serves 8

1 (10-ounce) can crushed pineapple
3 tablespoons reserved pineapple juice
1 (8-ounce) package cream cheese, softened
1 cup mayonnaise
¼ cup buttermilk
½ cup honey
1 cup finely chopped apricots
1 cup heavy cream
3 tablespoons powdered sugar
½ cup finely chopped toasted pecans

Thoroughly drain pineapple, reserving juice; set aside. In large bowl, beat cream cheese until light and fluffy. Gradually add mayonnaise and beat until very fluffy. Add buttermilk, pineapple juice, and honey and mix well until blended.

Add drained pineapple and chopped apricots to cream cheese mixture. In a small bowl, combine cream and powdered sugar and beat until stiff peaks form. Fold into cream cheese mixture along with pecans.

Spoon salad into paper-lined muffin cups and flash freeze in single layer until solid. Store in zipper-lock bags; label, seal bags, and freeze.

Before serving: Let salad stand at room temperature for 15 to 20 minutes.

My Immortal Ambrosia

Serves 6

1 (8-ounce) container frozen whipped topping, thawed
⅓ cup reserved pineapple juice
1 cup cottage cheese
2 (14-ounce) cans mandarin oranges, drained
1 (15-ounce) can crushed pineapple, drained, reserving juice
1 cup shredded coconut

In serving bowl, combine whipped topping, reserved pineapple juice, and cottage cheese; stir with wire whisk until blended.

Fold in remaining ingredients.

Cover and chill for 15 minutes before serving. Store leftovers in refrigerator.

TASTY TIDBIT

THE DESCRIPTIONS OF TRANSYLVANIA PRESENTED BY STOKER IN *DRACULA* WOULD HAVE MEANT LITTLE WITHOUT HIS INCLUSION OF THE FORBIDDING CARPATHIAN MOUNTAINS, WHICH RUN ALONG ITS BORDERS. RUNNING THROUGH CENTRAL AND EASTERN EUROPE FOR MORE THAN 600 MILES, THE CARPATHIANS ARE THE LARGEST MOUNTAIN CHAIN IN EUROPE, AND—PERFECT FOR THE APPREHENSIVE TONE OF STOKER'S NOVEL—ARE ALSO HOME TO THE LARGEST POPULATIONS OF BEARS, LYNXES, AND WOLVES.

Love at First Bite

Blood Orange Salad with Shrimp and Baby Spinach

Serves 4

2 bags baby spinach
2 blood oranges
1¼ pounds shrimp, peeled, deveined, cooked, and chilled
Juice of ½ a lemon
¼ cup extra-virgin olive oil
¼ teaspoon dry mustard
Salt and pepper to taste
¼ cup stemmed, loosely packed parsley or cilantro

Just before serving, place the spinach on individual serving plates.

Peel the oranges. Slice them crossways, about ¼" thick, picking out any seeds. Arrange on top of the spinach. Arrange the shrimp around the oranges.

Place the rest of the ingredients in the blender and purée until the dressing is a bright green. Pour over the salads. Serve chilled.

Be Still My Beeting Heart Salad

Serves 6

¼ cup red wine vinegar
1 teaspoon sugar
½ cup olive oil
1 teaspoon dried thyme or 1 tablespoon fresh thyme
1 teaspoon horseradish
Salt to taste
Freshly ground pepper to taste
6 cups red leaf lettuce, rinsed, drained, and torn to pieces
12 small red beets, roasted, skins peeled off, sliced
18 radishes, thinly sliced
1 red onion, thinly sliced

Whirl the red wine vinegar, sugar, olive oil, thyme, horseradish, salt, and pepper together in your blender. Set aside.

Arrange the red lettuce on serving plates. Add the beets, radishes, and onions.

Spoon the mixed dressing over the salads.

Vulgar Bulgur Salad
Serves 4

¾ cup fine-grain bulgur
1¼ cups boiling water
2 bunches scallions, finely sliced
2 small cucumbers, preferably Kirby, diced
1 bunch mint, rinsed and finely chopped
1 bunch parsley, rinsed and finely chopped
½ cup chopped dates
½ cup raisins
1 tablespoon olive oil, or more to taste
1 tablespoon lemon juice, or more to taste
Salt to taste

———— •◆•◆•◆• ————

Soak the cracked wheat in the boiling water and let it absorb the liquid for about 20 minutes. After that time, if any water remains, drain it off so the grains are plump but dry.

Meanwhile, combine the remaining ingredients in a large bowl, tossing to combine well. Add the bulgur and toss together well. Set aside for about 1 hour so the flavors can mingle.

Serves 4

⅓ cup oil
3 tablespoons apple cider vinegar
¼ cup sugar
½ teaspoon celery seed
¼ teaspoon salt
⅛ teaspoon pepper
2 apples, cored and sliced
4 cups butter lettuce, torn into bite-sized pieces
1 cup curly endive

In small bowl, combine oil, vinegar, sugar, celery seed, salt, and pepper and mix well with wire whisk to blend.

Place apples, lettuce, and endive in serving bowl and pour dressing over salad; toss gently to coat. Serve immediately.

TASTY TIDBIT

FRANZ ANTON MESMER DISCOVERED WHAT HE CALLED MAGNÉTISME ANIMAL (ANIMAL MAGNETISM), WHICH CAME TO BE CALLED MESMERISM. THE EVOLUTION OF HIS IDEAS AND PRACTICES LED TO THE DEVELOPMENT OF HYPNOTISM IN 1842. UNDER HYPNOSIS, PATIENTS IN TRANCE STATES HAVE BEEN KNOW TO COMMUNICATE WITH SPIRITS THROUGH SPEECH AND AUTOMATIC WRITING. VAMPIRES OFTEN CULL THEIR VICTIMS BY USING THESE PRACTICES.

Serves 6

1 blood orange, rind removed and cut into segments
½ cup pomegranate seeds
1 kiwifruit, peeled and cut into rounds
½ cup blueberries
½ cup quartered strawberries
½ cup fresh pineapple chunks
½ cup peeled mango chunks
¼ cup chopped candied ginger
¼ cup shredded coconut

Gently toss everything but the ginger and coconut in a large bowl.

Chill salad before serving.

Sprinkle the ginger and coconut on the salad and serve on individual plates or in one large bowl.

Skin Like Cellophane Noodle Salad
Serves 4

4 ounces cellophane, or bean thread, noodles,
softened in hot water for 20 minutes
1 (6-ounce) package of precooked chicken strips
½ cup thinly sliced scallions
½ cup fresh cilantro leaves
1–2 tablespoons crushed red peppers
2 tablespoons lime juice
2 tablespoons soy sauce
1 tablespoon pickled garlic, chopped
Sugar to taste

Drain the soaked and softened noodles and cut them into serving pieces. Put the noodles, chicken strips if using, scallions, cilantro leaves, and crushed red peppers into a serving bowl.

Mix together the lime juice, soy sauce, pickled garlic, and sugar and toss with the salad ingredients

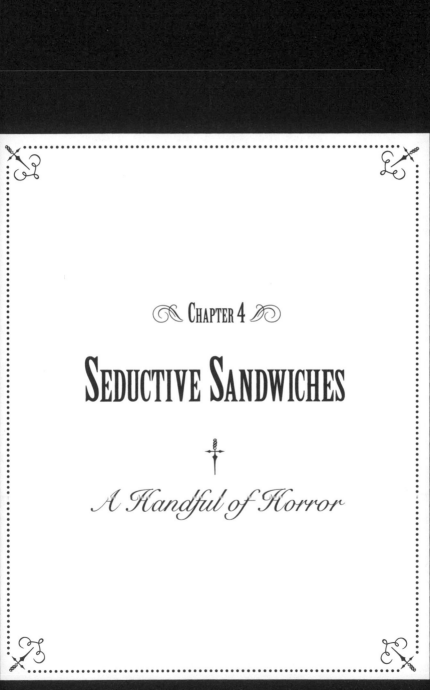

CHAPTER 4

SEDUCTIVE SANDWICHES

A Handful of Horror

Croak Monsieur

Serves 2

4 slices good-quality French bread
Unsalted butter
French-style grain mustard
4 slices good-quality ham
¼ cup plus 2 tablespoons Gruyère cheese, coarsely grated
4 cornichons, sliced
2 eggs, beaten

Butter both sides of each slice of bread. Spread generous amount of mustard on one side of two slices of bread, and top with sliced ham, ¼ cup grated cheese, sliced cornichons, and remaining slices of bread.

Grill sandwich under a broiler, in a sandwich grill, or in a heavy frying pan until both sides are golden brown and toasted.

Dip toasted sandwich in beaten eggs and fry both sides in a heavy frying pan over medium heat, until egg is cooked. Top with 1 tablespoon grated Gruyère on each sandwich, and serve immediately.

Grandpa Muenster's Avocado Hoagie
Serves 2–4

2 avocados
¼ cup creamy Italian salad dressing
2 hoagie buns, sliced and toasted
2 plum tomatoes, sliced
4 slices Muenster cheese

Preheat broiler. Peel and seed avocados; place in small bowl along with salad dressing. Mash, using a fork, until almost blended but with some pieces of avocado visible.

Place bottom halves of buns on broiler pan and spread with half of avocado mixture. Top with tomato slices and cover with cheese slices. Broil 6" from heat source for 2 to 5 minutes or until cheese is melted and begins to bubble. Spread top halves of buns with remaining avocado mixture and place on top of cheese. Serve immediately.

Not-So-Sloppy Josettes

8 servings

1 pound ground beef
1 onion, chopped
2 cups frozen hash brown potatoes
1 (15½-ounce) can sloppy joe sauce
8 hamburger buns

In a large skillet, brown the ground beef. Drain the extra fat from the ground beef.

Add the onions and potatoes. Pour the sloppy joe sauce over the top, stirring to blend the ingredients. Cover the skillet.

Reduce the heat to low and simmer for 30 minutes. Serve on hamburger buns.

TASTY TIDBIT

Josette Du Pres was the one true love of cursed vampire Barnabas Collins on the popular gothic soap opera *Dark Shadows*. Rather than succumb to a life as a vampire bride, Josette tragically chose to take her own life by jumping off the appropriately-named Widow's Hill.

Pâté of Prey Sandwich

Serves 1

3 cups shredded napa cabbage
1 jalapeño pepper, minced
1 teaspoon minced fresh gingerroot
2 tablespoons granulated sugar
¼ cup rice vinegar
2 tablespoons fresh cilantro leaves, chopped
Salt, to taste
2 long, soft rolls, split
8 ounces liver pâté or braunschweiger liverwurst

Mix together the cabbage, jalapeño, ginger, sugar, vinegar, cilantro, and some salt. Let stand for 30 minutes, then drain.

Toast the insides of the rolls, spread with the pâté, and top with the slaw.

Caught Red-Handed Tomato Sandwich

Serves 1

1 teaspoon extra-virgin olive oil, or more as desired
2 thick slices bread, preferably sourdough
1 teaspoon minced garlic
2 teaspoons mayonnaise, or more as desired
Fresh basil leaves
1 large heirloom tomato, thinly sliced
2 thin slices fresh mozzarella cheese
Salt and freshly ground black pepper to taste

Drizzle the olive oil on one of the slices of bread.

Mix together the garlic and mayonnaise and spread the mixture on the other slice.

Cover this slice with basil leaves. Top the leaves with the tomato and the mozzarella slices, layering the slices if necessary. Sprinkle the slices with salt and pepper and close the sandwich.

Love at First Bite

Finger Sandwiches

Serves 14

1 tablespoon butter
2 eggs
2 egg whites
3 tablespoons milk
⅛ teaspoon salt
⅛ teaspoon white pepper
½ cup plain low-fat yogurt
¼ cup nonfat mayonnaise
¼ cup nonfat sour cream
2 tablespoons Dijon mustard
3 large tomatoes
⅓ cup chopped flat-leaf parsley
12 slices firm whole-wheat sandwich bread

Melt butter in small saucepan over medium heat. Meanwhile, combine eggs, egg whites, milk, salt, and pepper in small bowl and beat well. Add to hot butter. Cook and stir over medium heat until eggs are set but still moist. Remove from heat.

Transfer eggs to a medium bowl and let cool. Using a knife, cut across the eggs to break them up. Stir in yogurt, mayonnaise, sour cream, and mustard and mix well.

Cut tomatoes in half and gently squeeze to seed. Chop coarsely. Add tomatoes and parsley to egg mixture and mix gently. Cover and chill for 3 hours. When ready to make sandwiches, cut the crusts off the sandwich bread and place on work surface.

Make sandwiches with the filling and the trimmed bread. Cut into 1" × 3" sandwiches using a very sharp knife. Cover and chill in refrigerator for 2 to 6 hours before serving.

Black and Blue Wraps
Serves 4

3 ounces cream cheese, at room temperature
1 tablespoon mayonnaise
2 ounces blue cheese crumbles
¼ teaspoon seasoned salt
Freshly cracked pepper, to taste
2 (8") low-carb tortillas, at room temperature
⅓ pound lean deli roast beef, trimmed of visible fat,
sliced, and cut into ½" strips
¼ cup diced roasted red pepper
1 cup chopped romaine hearts

Mix together the cream cheese, mayonnaise, blue cheese, salt, and pepper in a small bowl (or use a food processor to blend until smooth).

Place the tortillas on a clean work surface. Spread half of the cream cheese mixture on the upper third of each tortilla, about ½" from the edge. Place half of the roast beef on the lower third of each tortilla. Top each with peppers and lettuce.

Roll up each wrap: Starting from the bottom, fold the tortilla over the filling, compressing slightly to form a firm roll. Press at the top to "seal" the wrap closed with the cream cheese mixture. Cut the sandwich in half and wrap in plastic film. Refrigerate until ready to serve.

Love at First Bite

Sliced Open-Face Ham Sandwich

2 sandwiches

1 cup fresh bean sprouts
4 slices pumpernickel bread
4 teaspoons Dijon mustard
6 ounces thinly sliced deli ham
4 thin slices red onion
1 cup shredded mozzarella cheese

Rinse and drain the bean sprouts. Pat dry with a paper towel. Set aside.

Toast the bread. Spread 1 teaspoon mustard on each slice. Stack ham, bean sprouts, an onion slice, and ¼ of the cheese on each piece of bread.

Broil 4" to 6" from the heat, or microwave 2 sandwiches at a time on high, or toast in a toaster oven for 2 to 3 minutes until cheese melts and ingredients are heated through.

2–4 sandwiches

1 (8-ounce) package cream cheese
1 (6-ounce) can crabmeat (or flaked imitation crabmeat)
2 tablespoons dried parsley flakes
Seasoned salt, to taste
4 (1½"-thick) slices French bread

Let the cream cheese soften at room temperature for 10 or 15 minutes. Place in a medium-sized mixing bowl. Add the crabmeat, parsley, and seasoned salt. Stir until well blended.

Preheat oven to 400°F. Spread on one side of each French bread slice. Place on an ungreased baking sheet. Bake for 5 to 10 minutes.

2–4 sandwiches

½ eggplant (about 8 ounces)
1 medium zucchini
1 medium tomato
3 slices mozzarella cheese
⅓ cup bottled Italian salad dressing
4 slices Italian bread (¾" thick)
3 tablespoons mayonnaise
½ teaspoon dried basil

Rinse the eggplant and zucchini. Slice eggplant into 8 slices ¼" wide. Cut the zucchini in half horizontally. Cut each half in half lengthwise. Set aside. Slice the tomato horizontally into 8 slices. Set aside. Cut each cheese slice into 4 strips. Set aside.

Place eggplant and zucchini on a cookie sheet sprayed with non-stick cooking spray. Brush half of the salad dressing on the tops of the slices. Adjust top oven rack so it's 4" to 6" from the broiler. Cook 5 minutes. While the veggies are cooking, place mayonnaise and basil in a mixing bowl. Stir until blended. Set aside.

Remove sheet from oven. Turn vegetables cooked-side down. Brush uncooked side with remaining salad dressing. Broil 5 minutes until tender and slightly browned. Remove from oven and set aside.

Place bread on clean cookie sheet. Broil 2 minutes until lightly browned. Remove sheet from oven. Spread ¼ of mayonnaise mixture on each slice. Top with 2 slices each of eggplant, zucchini, and tomato. Top each sandwich with 3 slices of mozzarella. Return to the oven. Broil 1 to 2 minutes until cheese melts.

Sliced Open-Face Grilled Cheese and Pear Panini

Serves 6

1 pear
1 teaspoon lemon juice
1 cup water
6 large slices pumpernickel bread
1 tablespoon extra-virgin olive oil
6 thick slices Swiss cheese (1 ounce each)
Kosher salt, to taste
Fresh-cracked black pepper, to taste

Preheat broiler.

Dice the pear and toss it in the lemon juice and water; drain thoroughly.

Brush the bread with the oil and toast lightly. Place the cheese on the bread, sprinkle with diced pears, and season with salt and pepper.

Place under broiler until the cheese melts and the pears brown slightly, approximately 2 minutes.

Sliced Open-Face Turkey Sandwich
Serves 6

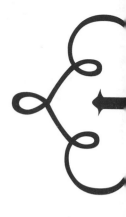

½ baguette
1 yellow onion
2 stalks celery
½ cup mushrooms
1 tablespoon olive oil
6 ounces turkey gravy
2 ounces warm turkey
Fresh-cracked black pepper, to taste
Kosher salt, to taste

Slice the baguette in half lengthwise. Slice the onion and finely slice the celery and mushrooms.

Heat the oil to medium temperature in a small saucepan, then add the onions, celery, and mushrooms. Cover and simmer at medium-low heat until the vegetables are wilted.

Heat the gravy. Place the cooked vegetables on the baguette and layer with warm turkey. Season with pepper and salt to taste.

To serve, cut into 6 portions and ladle with gravy.

Sliced Open-Face London Broil

Serves 6

1 pound London broil
¼ cup mustard
Fresh-cracked black pepper, to taste
6 slices hearty grain bread
1 tablespoon extra-virgin olive oil
½ cup brown gravy
¼ cup horseradish
6 cups mixed salad greens

Preheat grill or broiler.

Rub the steak with mustard and season with pepper. Grill to desired doneness. Let rest for 2 minutes, then slice thinly on bias.

While the steak cooks, toast the bread and brush with oil. Heat the gravy.

To serve, layer the meat on the bread with horseradish and drizzle with gravy. Serve over mixed greens.

TASTY TIDBIT

ODDLY ENOUGH, THERE DOESN'T SEEM TO BE AN EXPERT CONSENSUS AS TO WHAT A GROUP OF VAMPIRES IS CALLED. THROUGHOUT FILM AND BOTH FICTION AND NONFICTION WRITINGS THEY'RE VARIOUSLY REFERRED TO AS A *CLUTCH*, A *BROOD*, OR A *COVEN*. IN FOLKLORE, THEY'RE OFTEN REFERRED TO AS A *PACK*, WHILE IN SOME ARENAS THEY ARE ALSO KNOWN AS A *CLAN* OR ARE DIVIDED INTO *BLOODLINES*.

Love at First Bite

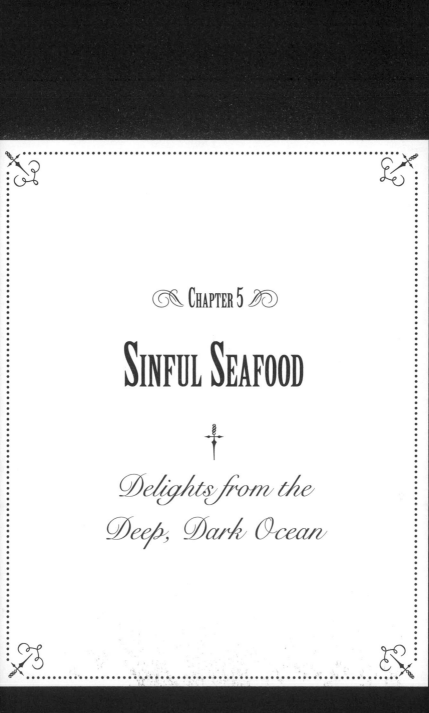

CHAPTER 5

SINFUL SEAFOOD

Delights from the
Deep, Dark Ocean

Sookie's Shrimp Scampi Kabobs

Serves 6

3 lemons
¼ cup olive oil
4 cloves garlic, minced
1 teaspoon dried thyme leaves
½ teaspoon salt
⅛ teaspoon white pepper
1½ pounds large raw shrimp, cleaned
18 large mushrooms
2 yellow squash, cut into 1" pieces

Prepare and preheat grill. Using lemon zester, remove peel from 1 of the lemons. Place in medium bowl. Squeeze juice from the peeled lemon and add to peel in bowl. Cut remaining lemons into 6 wedges each and set aside. Add oil, garlic, thyme, salt, and pepper to lemon mixture in bowl and mix well. Add shrimp and let stand for 10 minutes.

Drain shrimp, reserving marinade. Place shrimp, mushrooms, squash pieces, and lemon wedges alternately on twelve 8"-long metal skewers. Brush skewers with marinade, then grill 4 to 6 inches from medium-hot coals for 8 to 14 minutes, turning once, until shrimp are curled and pink and vegetables are tender. Brush skewers often with marinade. Discard any remaining marinade.

Love at First Bite

Bon Temps Fish

Serves 6

½ cup chili sauce
1½ cups pasta sauce
2 cups medium cooked shrimp
2 tablespoons olive oil
6 (4- to 6-ounce) mild white fish fillets
½ teaspoon salt
⅛ teaspoon red pepper flakes
2 tablespoons lemon juice

Preheat oven to 450°F. In medium saucepan, combine chili sauce and pasta sauce; bring to a boil over medium-high heat. Reduce heat to medium and simmer for 5 minutes, stirring frequently. Stir in shrimp, cover, and remove from heat.

Meanwhile, place oil in glass baking dish. Arrange fish in dish and sprinkle with salt, pepper flakes, and lemon juice. Bake for 8 to 10 minutes or until fish flakes easily when tested with a fork. Place on serving dish and top with shrimp sauce. Serve immediately.

Salem's Lot Salmon

Serves 4

4 (6-ounce) salmon fillets
1 teaspoon salt
⅛ teaspoon white pepper
½ teaspoon dried Italian seasoning
2 tablespoons olive oil
1 (10-ounce) jar Alfredo sauce
1 cup frozen chopped spinach, thawed and well drained
½ cup grated Parmesan cheese

Preheat broiler. Sprinkle salmon with salt, pepper, and Italian seasoning and drizzle with olive oil. Place on broiler pan and let stand.

In large skillet, heat Alfredo sauce over medium-low heat until bubbly. Place salmon fillets under broiler 4" to 6" from heat source for 5 minutes. Stir spinach into Alfredo sauce and let simmer over low heat. Turn salmon fillets and broil for 3 to 4 minutes longer, until salmon is almost done.

Place salmon on ovenproof serving platter and top with sauce mixture. Sprinkle with Parmesan cheese. Broil for 2 to 4 minutes, until cheese melts and begins to brown. Serve immediately.

TASTY TIDBIT

ALTHOUGH STEPHEN KING ORIGINALLY CALLED THE TOWN "JERUSALEM'S LOT," THE PUBLISHER SHORTENED THE TITLE TO *SALEM'S LOT* BECAUSE THEY FELT THE ORIGINAL TITLE CARRIED A RELIGIOUS CONNOTATION.

Love at First Bite

Violent Shrimp Tempura

Serves 4

¾ cup beer
¾ cup all-purpose flour
¾ teaspoon salt
4 cups vegetable oil for deep-frying
24 large uncooked shrimp, shelled and deveined

Whisk beer into flour until smooth. Stir in salt.

Heat 4 cups vegetable oil in a 6-quart soup pot or a deep fryer to 375°F.

Dip shrimp individually in batter. Let excess batter drip off, and then carefully drop the shrimp into the hot oil.

Cook battered shrimp about 3 minutes. Remove from oil using tongs or a slotted spoon.

Drain on paper towels or brown paper; serve immediately.

Muscles in Creamy Leek Sauce
Serves 4

2 tablespoons butter
1 cup sliced leeks, rinsed well, white and light green parts only
3 pounds mussels
1 cup dry white wine
1 cup heavy cream
½ cup bottled clam juice
2 tablespoons chopped fresh thyme
¼ teaspoon kosher salt
Freshly cracked black pepper, to taste

Melt the butter in a heavy-bottomed saucepan with tight-fitting lid. Add the leeks and cook until soft, about 5 minutes, uncovered and stirring frequently. Add the mussels, then the wine, cream, clam juice, and half of the thyme. Lightly season with salt and pepper.

Bring to a simmer, reduce heat, and cover pan. Cook until the mussels open, about 5 minutes. Shake the pan occasionally throughout the cooking process.

Equally divide the mussels between 4 shallow bowls. Discard any mussels that have not opened. Add the remaining thyme to the broth, taste, and adjust seasoning as desired. Bring the broth to a simmer and drizzle over the mussels. Serve hot.

Love at First Bite

The Count's Calamari

Serves 4

1 cup flour
1 teaspoon salt
1 teaspoon paprika
½ teaspoon pepper
4 cups vegetable oil for deep-frying
2 pounds thawed calamari, cut into rings
Lemon wedges

Mix flour with salt, paprika, and pepper.

Heat 4 cups vegetable oil in a 6-quart soup pot or a deep fryer to 365°F.

Toss a handful of calamari in flour mixture and shake off excess.

Deep fry until golden brown, about 3 minutes. Drain on paper towels.

Repeat with remaining calamari. Serve immediately with lemon wedges to sprinkle calamari with lemon juice.

TASTY TIDBIT

MOST OF US GREW UP COUNTING BATS WITH COUNT VON COUNT, THE FAMED SESAME STREET MUPPET. TWO BATS . . . AH, AH, AH.

Chupacabra Tacos

Serves 4

8 corn tortillas
1 pound firm white fish such as halibut or snapper
½ cup cornmeal
1 tablespoon olive oil
Lime wedges
1 cup shredded purple cabbage
1 cup salsa
¼ cup diced avocados
¼ cup sour cream

Warm tortillas wrapped in paper towels in microwave. Discard paper towels and wrap in foil to keep them warm.

Cut the fish into strips, dredge in cornmeal, and sear in olive oil for about 5 minutes.

Break the cooked fish into chunks; and put chunks in warm tortillas.

Squeeze a lime wedge on the fish, then top with cabbage, salsa, avocados, and sour cream.

TASTY TIDBIT

BLOODY ATTACKS ON LIVESTOCK IN PUERTO RICO, MEXICO, TEXAS, AND AS FAR NORTH AS MAINE HAVE BEEN ATTRIBUTED TO THE ELUSIVE CHUPACABRA (WHICH MEANS "GOAT SUCKER") AND HAVE TRIGGERED MEDIA HYSTERICS, A HANDFUL OF FANCIFUL HORROR FILMS, AND APPEARANCES ON SERIAL TELEVISION DRAMAS SUCH AS *THE X-FILES*.

Love at First Bite

The Volturi's Italian Baked Fish

Serves 4

1 pound (16 ounces) cod fillets
1 (14½-ounce) can stewed tomatoes
¼ teaspoon dried minced onion
½ teaspoon dried minced garlic
¼ teaspoon dried basil
¼ teaspoon dried parsley
⅛ teaspoon dried oregano
⅛ teaspoon sugar
1 tablespoon grated Parmesan cheese

Preheat oven to 375°F. Rinse the cod with cold water and pat dry with paper towels.

In a 2- to 3-quart baking pan or casserole treated with nonstick cooking spray, combine all the ingredients except the fish, and mix. Arrange the fillets over the tomato mixture, folding thin tail ends under to give the fillets an even thickness; spoon some of the tomato mixture over the fillets, if desired. For fillets about 1" thick, bake uncovered for 20 to 25 minutes, or until the fish is opaque and flaky.

Lucy's Lobster Rolls

Serves 4

4 hot dog buns
2 tablespoons soft butter
1 cup cooked lobster meat chunks
¼ cup mayonnaise
¼ cup diced celery
Salt and pepper to taste

Butter the insides of the buns and toast them on a griddle or skillet.

Combine lobster meat, mayonnaise, celery, salt, and pepper, and mix well.

Spoon lobster salad onto toasted buns.

TASTY TIDBIT

IN BRAM STOKER'S *DRACULA*, LUCY WESTENRA IS ONE OF DRACULA'S VICTIMS. SHE WAS TRANSFORMED INTO A VAMPIRE BY DRACULA AND THEN STAKED TO DEATH BY HER FIANCÉ, ARTHUR HOLMWOOD.

Love at First Bite

Collinwood Crab Cakes

Serves 4

1 pound crabmeat (fresh or canned is fine)
½ cup mayonnaise
¼ cup diced red bell pepper
¼ cup sliced whole green onions
1 tablespoon lemon juice
1 slice white bread, soaked in milk and squeezed dry
Salt and pepper, to taste
1 egg, beaten
2 cups dry bread crumbs
Butter to sauté crab cakes

Combine crabmeat, mayonnaise, red bell pepper, green onions, lemon juice, and bread in a bowl until well mixed. Season with salt and pepper.

Put the egg in one bowl and bread crumbs in another. Shape crab mixture into patties or cakes and dip them first in egg, then in bread crumbs.

Fry the crab cakes in butter until browned on both sides. Serve warm.

TASTY TIDBIT

COLLINWOOD IS HOME TO BARNABAS COLLINS, THE BLOOD-SUCKING STAR OF GOTHIC SOAP OPERA *DARK SHADOWS*. POPULAR IN THE SIXTIES AND SEVENTIES, *DARK SHADOWS* IS GETTING A FACE LIFT AND MOVING TO THE SILVER SCREEN IN 2011 WITH TIM BURTON AS THE DIRECTOR AND JOHNNY DEPP AS BARNABAS.

Deviled Crab

Serves 4

1 pound crabmeat
½ cup dry bread crumbs
½ cup béchamel sauce
¼ cup heavy cream
1 teaspoon cayenne pepper sauce
1 egg
1 clove garlic, minced
¼ cup chopped green bell pepper
Salt and pepper
2 tablespoons butter

Preheat oven to 400°F. Butter a 2-quart baking dish.

Combine crabmeat, bread crumbs, béchamel sauce, heavy cream, cayenne pepper sauce, egg, garlic, and green bell pepper until thoroughly mixed.

Season with salt and pepper and put mixture into buttered baking dish.

Bake for 15 minutes, or until browned and bubbly.

Teriyaki Shrimp Teaser

Serves 1

1 cup peeled and deveined frozen small shrimp
¼ cup soy sauce
1 tablespoon, plus 1 teaspoon cooking sherry
1½ teaspoons granulated sugar
1 tablespoon vegetable oil

Place the shrimp under cold, running water for at least 5 minutes until thawed. Drain and pat dry on paper towels.

Combine the soy sauce, cooking sherry, and sugar in a small bowl. Pour the marinade into a large resealable plastic bag, or split equally into two smaller resealable plastic bags. Place the shrimp in the marinade and move the bag around to make sure all the shrimp are covered. Refrigerate for 30 minutes.

Heat the oil in a frying pan. Sauté the shrimp until they turn pink. Serve hot.

Cordelia's Tuna Noodle Casserole

Serves 6

8 ounces egg noodles, cooked
1 cup sliced mushrooms
2 tablespoons butter
2 tablespoons all-purpose flour
2 cups milk
2 cans tuna, drained
¾ cup frozen peas
Salt and pepper to taste
1 cup crushed potato chips

Preheat oven to 375°F and butter a 9" × 13" casserole dish. Lay cooked noodles in the dish.

Sauté mushrooms in butter, sprinkle with flour, and cook for a few minutes. Add milk, and cook until thickened. Stir in tuna and peas. Season with salt and pepper.

Pour mushroom sauce mixture over noodles and gently toss if necessary to distribute evenly.

Sprinkle potato chips over the top and bake for 20 minutes.

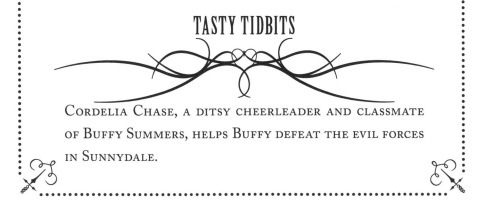

TASTY TIDBITS

CORDELIA CHASE, A DITSY CHEERLEADER AND CLASSMATE OF BUFFY SUMMERS, HELPS BUFFY DEFEAT THE EVIL FORCES IN SUNNYDALE.

The Slayer's Scallops and Shrimp with White Bean Sauce

Serves 4

1 small white onion
2 garlic cloves
1⅓ cups canned white beans
½ pound medium-sized shrimp
2 teaspoons olive oil, divided
¼ cup dry white wine
¼ tightly packed cup fresh parsley leaves
¼ lightly packed cup fresh basil leaves
¼ cup chicken broth
½ pound scallops

Chop the onion into ¼" pieces. Mince the garlic. Drain and rinse the beans. Parboil the shrimp. Remove the shells and devein the shrimp.

In a medium-sized saucepan, sauté the onion and garlic in 1 teaspoon of the olive oil over low heat until the onion is soft. Add the wine and simmer the mixture until the wine is reduced by half. Add the parsley, basil, ⅓ cup of the beans, and the chicken broth. Simmer the mixture for 1 minute, stirring constantly.

Transfer the bean mixture to a blender or food processor and purée it. Pour the purée back into the saucepan and add the remaining beans. Simmer for 2 minutes.

Heat the remaining 1 teaspoon of oil over high heat in a medium-sized skillet until it is hot. Sauté the shrimp for 2 minutes on each side.

Using a slotted spoon, transfer the shrimp to a plate and cover to keep warm. Add the scallops to the skillet and sauté them for 1 minute on each side. To serve, divide the bean sauce between four shallow bowls and arrange the shellfish over the top.

Serves 4

1 pound sea scallops

2 large carrots

3 garlic cloves

3 green onions

6 ounces fresh snap peas

8 ounces fettuccine

2 tablespoons olive oil

1 tablespoon butter

½ cup dry white wine

⅓ cup water

1 tablespoon fresh dill

1 teaspoon instant chicken bouillon granules

¼ teaspoon crushed red pepper

2 tablespoons cornstarch

2 tablespoons cold water

¼ cup grated Parmesan cheese

½ teaspoon freshly cracked black pepper

Thaw the scallops if frozen. Cut any large scallops in half and set aside. Peel and thinly slice the carrots. Peel and mince the garlic cloves. Peel and thinly slice the green onions. Remove the stems from the snap peas.

Cook the fettuccine in boiling water with 1 tablespoon of the olive oil until al dente. Drain, toss with the butter, and set aside.

Pour the remaining oil into a wok or large skillet. Preheat over medium-high heat. Add the carrots and garlic; stir-fry for 4 minutes. Add the green onions and snap peas; stir-fry for 2 to 3 minutes or until crisp. Remove the vegetables and set aside.

Reduce heat to low and let the wok cool for 1 minute. Carefully add the wine, the ⅓ cup water, the dill, bouillon granules, and crushed red pepper to the wok. Add the scallops. Simmer, uncovered, for 1 to 2 minutes or until the scallops are opaque, stirring often.

Stir together the cornstarch and 2 tablespoons cold water. Add to the wok. Cook and stir until the mixture is thickened and bubbly. Return the vegetables to the wok. Add the pasta and toss to mix. Heat through.

Transfer to dinner plates. Sprinkle with Parmesan cheese and cracked black pepper.

TASTY TIDBIT
WHAT DO VAMPIRES LOAD ON iTUNES?

"BELA LUGOSI'S DEAD" BY THE BAUHAUS

"BLOODLETTING" BY CONCRETE BLONDE

"LIVING DEAD GIRL" BY ROB ZOMBIE

"VAMPIRES WILL NEVER HURT YOU"
BY MY CHEMICAL ROMANCE

"DRACULA'S WEDDING" BY OUTKAST

"LOVE SONG FOR A VAMPIRE" BY ANNIE LENNOX

"VAMPIRE BLUES" BY NEIL YOUNG

"DRACULA MOON" BY JOAN OSBORNE

"NOSFERATU" BY BLUE OYSTER CULT

"BULLET WITH BUTTERFLY WINGS"
BY SMASHING PUMPKINS

Muscles Marinara

Serves 6

1½ dozen mussels
2 shallots
3 cloves garlic
6 plum tomatoes
1 anchovy fillet
1 tablespoon olive oil
1 cup dry red wine
½ cup fish stock
¼ teaspoon dried red pepper flakes
1 teaspoon dried oregano

Thoroughly clean the mussels. Dice the shallots and mince the garlic. Roughly chop the tomatoes. Mash the anchovy.

Heat the oil to medium temperature in a large saucepot. Add the shallots, garlic, and tomatoes; sweat for 5 minutes. Add the mussels, wine, stock, pepper flakes, and oregano; simmer until the mussels open.

Discard any mussels that have not opened. Ladle into serving bowls and top with mashed anchovy.

Love at First Bite

Bill Compton's Snow Crab

Serves 6

6 snow crab claw clusters
2 pounds parsnips
6 celery stalks
1 yellow onion
½ bunch fresh parsley
½ cup white wine (Pinot Grigio or Sauvignon Blanc)
Juice of 1 lemon
1 cup fish stock
3 bay leaves

Clean the crab legs thoroughly in ice-cold water. Peel and roughly chop the parsnips. Chop the celery, onion, and parsley.

Combine all the ingredients except the snow crab in a medium-sized saucepot and bring to a boil; reduce to a simmer and cook uncovered for approximately 20 to 30 minutes.

Add the crab legs and cook for 10 to 15 minutes, until the crab is cooked. Remove the bay leaves, then serve.

TASTY TIDBIT

BILL COMPTON, THE 173-YEAR-OLD VAMPIRE, IS IN LOVE WITH SOOKIE STACKHOUSE. OF COURSE, THE FACT THAT BILL IS 148 YEARS OLDER THAN SOOKIE MATTERS LITTLE, CONSIDERING THAT VAMPIRES, COURTESY OF THE INVENTION OF SYNTHETIC BLOOD, HAVE NOW BECOME ACCEPTED IN SOCIETY.

No Soul with Lemon and Capers

Serves 6

3 cloves garlic
3 sprigs fresh dill, leaves only
1½ pounds sole
Fresh-cracked black pepper, to taste
1 teaspoon fresh-grated lemon zest
1 teaspoon olive oil
½ teaspoon capers

Preheat oven broiler. Mince the garlic and chop the dill.

Place the sole on a broiler pan; sprinkle with pepper, zest, and garlic, and drizzle with the oil. Place under broiler for 3 minutes, then turn carefully and broil for 1 minute longer.

Remove from broiler and top with dill and capers.

TASTY TIDBIT

ONE THEORY OF WHY GARLIC REPELS VAMPIRES IS BORN OF THE SIMILARITY BETWEEN VAMPIRES AND MOSQUITOES, BOTH OF WHICH BITE THEIR VICTIMS AND DRINK THEIR BLOOD AND BOTH OF WHOM CAN SPREAD DISEASE THROUGH THEIR BITES. GARLIC HAS BEEN KNOWN TO REPEL MOSQUITOES AND OTHER INSECTS. AS OF THIS WRITING, HOWEVER, NO ONE HAS AS YET MANUFACTURED A BUG SPRAY FOR VAMPIRES.

Blackened and Blue Tilapia

Serves 6

1½ pounds fresh tilapia
¼ teaspoon cayenne pepper
¼ teaspoon chili powder
Fresh-cracked black pepper, to taste
1 tablespoon olive oil
3 ounces blue cheese

Rinse the fish in ice water and pat dry. Sift together the cayenne, chili powder, and black pepper; season the fish with the mixture.

Heat the oil to medium temperature in a medium-sized skillet; sauté the fish on each side until crispy, golden brown, and flaky. Drain on paper-toweled rack.

To serve, plate the drained fish and sprinkle with blue cheese.

Beer "Bat"tered Fish

Serves 4

1½ pounds cod or other firm white fish
1¾ cups flour
1 teaspoon salt
½ teaspoon pepper
1½ teaspoons baking powder
6 ounces dark beer
⅓ cup milk
2 egg yolks
2 egg whites
4 cups peanut oil

Cut the fish into planks about 2" wide and 3" long.

Combine ¾ cup flour, salt, pepper, and baking powder. Gradually whisk in beer, then milk, then egg yolks.

Beat egg whites to stiff peaks, then fold them into the batter.

Dip each fish piece in flour (remaining 1 cup), then dip in batter.

Fry fish in batches in oil heated to 365°F in a large pot or deep fryer, immediately after dipping them in batter, for about 5 minutes. Check one to see if the fish is done before removing all of them. The fish will flake apart with a fork when done. Drain on paper towels and serve hot.

Love at First Bite

Louis's Dungeon Crab

Serves 4

2 hard-boiled eggs, peeled
2 Roma tomatoes
¼ cup cocktail sauce or ketchup
½ cup mayonnaise
1 tablespoon heavy cream
Dash of Tabasco sauce
1 tablespoon chopped parsley
1 tablespoon minced green bell pepper
1 tablespoon minced green onions
1 teaspoon lemon juice
2 cups shredded iceberg lettuce
1 pound Dungeness crabmeat

Cut the eggs and tomatoes into quarters, then set aside.

Mix the cocktail sauce, mayonnaise, cream, Tabasco, parsley, bell pepper, green onions, and lemon juice together to make the pink Louis dressing.

Divide the lettuce among four plates. Place a mound of crabmeat on each plate of lettuce. Pour the dressing over the crabmeat.

TASTY TIDBIT

THIS DISH IS A VERSION OF CRAB LOUIS WHICH WAS INVENTED IN THE LATE 1800S ON THE WEST COAST. IF ANNE RICE'S FAMOUS TORTURED VAMPIRE LOUIS WERE HUMAN AT THAT TIME, HE WOULD HAVE LOVED THIS DISH.

Stone-Dead Crab Claws

Serves 4

8 stone-crab claws, thawed
½ cup mayonnaise
3 tablespoons Dijon mustard

To thaw the frozen stone-crab claws, place in the refrigerator for 12 to 18 hours.

Combine the mayonnaise and Dijon mustard.

Crack the claws with a mallet and serve chilled with the mayonnaise mustard sauce for dipping.

TASTY TIDBIT

A threshold, meaning the bottom of a doorway or entrance, holds significance to vampires. In general, a bloodsucker is not allowed to cross a threshold unless invited to do so. Of course, once you've invited the devil inside your domicile, there is no looking back.

Blood-Red Snapper Veracruz

Serves 6

6 (6-ounce) red snapper fillets
2 tablespoons lime juice
1 tablespoon chili powder
1 teaspoon salt
2 tablespoons butter
1 tablespoon oil
1 onion, sliced
4 cloves garlic, minced
1 serrano pepper, minced
4 tomatoes, seeded and diced
2 tablespoons tomato paste
½ teaspoon dried oregano
2 tablespoons tequila
⅓ cup sliced green olives
1 tablespoon capers
¼ cup chopped cilantro
1 avocado, sliced

Preheat oven to 350°F. Place snapper in glass baking dish in single layer; sprinkle with lime juice, chili powder, and salt; set aside.

In heavy skillet, melt butter and oil over medium heat and cook onion, garlic, and serrano pepper until crisp-tender, about 4 to 5 minutes. Add tomatoes, tomato paste, oregano, and tequila; simmer for 5 to 10 minutes over medium heat. Stir in olives and capers; pour over red snapper in baking dish.

Bake at 350°F for 12 to 18 minutes or until fish flakes when tested with fork. Sprinkle fish with cilantro and garnish with avocado; serve immediately.

Sunnydale's Seafood Stir-Fry

Serves 2–4

3 tablespoons vegetable oil
3 teaspoons garlic, chopped
2 shallots, chopped
1 stalk lemongrass, bruised
¼ cup chopped basil
1 can bamboo shoots, rinsed and drained
3 tablespoons fish sauce
Pinch of brown sugar
1 pound fresh shrimp, scallops, or other seafood, cleaned
2–4 servings of rice, cooked according to package directions

Heat the oil in a skillet or wok over high heat. Add the garlic, shallots, lemongrass, and basil, and sauté for 1 to 2 minutes.

Reduce heat, add the remaining ingredients, except the rice, and stir-fry until the seafood is done to your liking, approximately 5 minutes. Serve over rice.

TASTY TIDBIT

Sunnydale, California, the stomping grounds of Buffy, Angel, and Spike, is one messed-up town. As the location of a "Hellmouth," or portal between two worlds, this normally quiet suburb sees a lot of action once the slayer arrives.

Blackened Like My Heart Bass

Serves 4–6

2 pounds bass fillets
¼ cup plus 1 tablespoon vegetable oil
1 tablespoon lemon pepper
1 tablespoon paprika
2 teaspoons garlic salt
2 teaspoons dried basil
2 teaspoons dried oregano
2 teaspoons red pepper
2 teaspoons freshly ground black pepper
¼ cup oil

Rinse fish fillets and pat dry. Place in a bowl and lightly toss with 1 tablespoon of vegetable oil. Set aside.

Combine lemon pepper, paprika, garlic salt, basil, oregano, red pepper, and black pepper in a bowl. Whisk to blend well. Transfer to a larger shallow bowl.

Add ¼ cup oil to a cast-iron skillet and place over high heat.

Dredge each fillet in the spice mixture, lightly coating both sides of the fillet.

Sear a batch of several fillets at a time in the hot skillet. Cook for about 1 to 1½ minutes per side. Fillets should be crusty. Continue cooking batches of fillets until done.

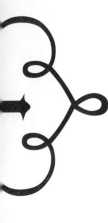

Luscious Lobster Risotto
Serves 6

1 medium yellow onion
1 shallot
3 cloves garlic
½ bunch parsley
2 teaspoons extra-virgin olive oil
1½ cups Arborio rice
¼ cup dry white wine
3½ cups fish stock
1½ pounds cooked lobster
¼ cup grated Asiago cheese

Dice the onion and shallot. Mince the garlic. Chop the parsley.

Heat the oil to medium temperature in a medium-sized frying pan; sauté the onion for 2 minutes. Add the shallot, and sauté for 1 minute more. Add the garlic, and sauté for 1 more minute.

Add the rice and mix well with the sautéed mixture. Pour in the wine and let reduce by half.

Add the stock, ½ cup at a time, stirring until each is fully incorporated before adding more. Continue the process until all stock is incorporated and the rice is thoroughly cooked.

Remove from heat. Stir in the cooked lobster and cheese. Sprinkle with parsley and serve.

Love at First Bite

Monster Mash Salmon Hash

Serves 6

¾ pound fresh salmon fillet
½ teaspoon salt
½ teaspoon ground black pepper
2–3 medium-sized russet potatoes
2 tablespoons lemon juice
2 cups cold water
6 tablespoons clarified butter
¾ cup sliced yellow bell pepper

¾ cup sliced red bell pepper
1 large sliced yellow onion
¾ cup sliced leeks (white part only)
1 tablespoon chopped parsley
½ teaspoon chopped thyme
½ teaspoon minced savory
½ teaspoon minced tarragon
2 tablespoons unsalted butter

Remove the skin from the salmon fillet and cut the fish into 12 pieces. Season with salt and pepper, and refrigerate. Peel and shred the potatoes.

Combine the lemon juice and cold water in a large bowl. Place the potatoes in the lemon water. Just before frying, drain and squeeze out excess liquid from the potatoes.

In a large skillet, heat the clarified butter and spread the potatoes loosely and evenly on the bottom of the pan. Brown the potatoes and drain on paper towels. Set aside and keep warm.

Pour out all but 1 tablespoon of the butter from the pan. Add the bell peppers, onion, and leek. Sauté for 3 to 4 minutes or until the vegetables are softened. Stir in the herbs. Stir in the potatoes. Keep warm.

Melt the unsalted butter in a skillet over high heat and sauté the salmon until golden brown, about 2 minutes. Do not allow the pieces of salmon to touch or they will steam and not sear. Turn the salmon over and add the potato mixture to the skillet. Cook for an additional 1 to 2 minutes.

The Cullens's Catfish with Fried Green Tomatoes

Serves 4

¾ cup mayonnaise
Zest and juice of 1 lemon
1 clove garlic, minced
1 cup cornmeal
½ cup flour
1 teaspoon salt
1 teaspoon pepper
½ cup vegetable oil or more
2 large green tomatoes
2 pounds catfish fillets, skinless

Combine mayonnaise, lemon, and garlic in a bowl and whisk to blend. Set aside.

Combine cornmeal, flour, salt, and pepper in a bowl large enough for dredging.

Heat vegetable oil in a large skillet over medium-high heat.

Slice green tomatoes ½" thick and dredge in cornmeal mixture. Place in the skillet and cook until brown on each side, about 3 or 4 minutes per side. Remove and keep warm.

Dredge the catfish fillets in the cornmeal mixture. Place in the skillet and fry until golden brown, about 3 or 4 minutes per side, depending on how thick the fillets are. Add more oil as needed. Serve catfish and tomatoes with the mayonnaise sauce on the side.

Love at First Bite

Rosalie's Roasted Red Snapper
Serves 4

2 large red onions, peeled and sliced
½ cup mixed herbs, chopped
(chives, basil, tarragon, thyme, and so on)
1 cup fresh or canned tomatoes, chopped
½ cup niçoise or kalamata olives, pitted
1 large whole red snapper, about 2 pounds, cleaned
½ cup olive oil

Preheat the oven to 450°F.

In a casserole or gratin dish large enough to hold the fish, arrange the onions, chopped herbs, tomatoes, and olives.

Rinse the snapper under cold, running water and pat dry. Place the snapper on top of the onion mixture and drizzle with olive oil.

Tent the fish with aluminum foil and roast for 20 to 22 minutes or until the fish begins to flake when tested in the thickest part.

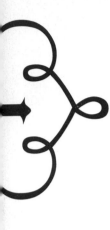

Selene's Smoked Salmon
Serves 4–6

1 lemon, sliced
6–8 sprigs fresh thyme
4 cloves garlic, sliced
1 (3- to 4-pound) salmon, cleaned and dressed
3 tablespoons butter
1 cup dry white wine
¼ cup lemon juice
½ teaspoon red pepper flakes

Place lemon slices, sprigs of thyme, and sliced garlic in the cavity of the salmon. Place the salmon in a disposable aluminum pan that will fit in your smoker or grill.

Melt the butter in a saucepan and add the wine, lemon juice, and red pepper flakes. Simmer for about 2 or 3 minutes. Pour the liquid over the salmon and cover tightly with foil. Let sit.

Prepare a 225°F fire in a smoker or grill. Place 3 chunks of wood such as oak or apple on the fire. Place the pan of salmon in the smoker or on the indirect-heat side of the grill. Close the lid.

Smoke for 1 hour. Then unwrap the foil and smoke for another hour.

TASTY TIDBIT

PORTRAYED BY KATE BECKINSALE IN *UNDERWORLD*, THE VAMPIRE SELENE IS MORE THAN JUST YOUR AVERAGE BLOODSUCKING VIXEN. SHE EPITOMIZES NEW-AGE GIRL POWER, CASTING HERSELF IN THE MIDDLE OF A DEADLY WAR BETWEEN VAMPIRES AND LYCANS.

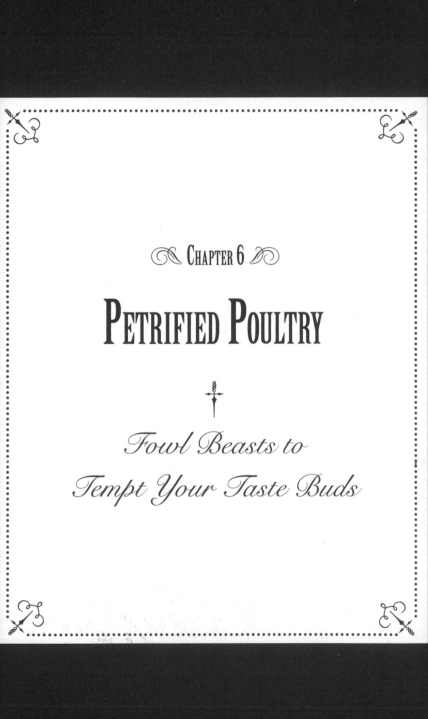

Chapter 6

Petrified Poultry

Fowl Beasts to Tempt Your Taste Buds

Buffalo Bat Wings

Serves 6

1 cup all-purpose flour
1 teaspoon salt
3 pounds chicken wings
1 cup butter, melted
1 teaspoon garlic powder
1 tablespoon Worcestershire sauce
½ cup cayenne pepper sauce

Preheat oven to 375°F. Combine the flour and salt in a large bowl. Toss chicken wings in flour mixture.

Shake off excess flour and put the wings on a foil-lined cookie sheet. Repeat in batches.

Bake wings for 30 minutes; turn over and bake another 15 minutes.

In a large bowl, combine butter, garlic powder, Worcestershire sauce, and cayenne pepper sauce.

Remove wings from oven; toss in the large bowl with sauce. Return coated wings to cookie sheet; bake for 15 minutes more.

TASTY TIDBIT

THE BAT HAS APPEARED IN LEGEND FOR CENTURIES, BUT DIDN'T BECOME FAMOUS UNTIL BRAM STOKER BROUGHT IT TO THE FOREFRONT. STOKER MADE FREE USE OF THE BAT IN *DRACULA*, AS IT APPEARED IN THE WINDOWS OF RENFIELD, LUCY, AND THE HARKERS. AFTER APPEARING IN LUGOSI'S *DRACULA*, IT QUICKLY BECAME ONE OF THE MOST DEFINITIVE ICONS OF THE VAMPIRE.

Love at First Bite

Fall-Off-the-Bone Chicken

Serves 4

1 (4-pound) roasting chicken, rinsed, giblet pack removed
Salt and pepper
1 bay leaf
1 onion, quartered
1 tablespoon paprika
1 teaspoon herbs de Provence or dried thyme
1 teaspoon each salt and pepper

Preheat oven to 400°F. Season inside of bird with salt and pepper, then put bay leaf and onion inside. Tuck wings under the back of the bird.

Mix together paprika, herbs, 1 teaspoon each salt and pepper, and rub the mixture all over the chicken's skin. Place chicken in a roasting pan, breast-side up.

Roast the chicken uncovered in the oven until you can move the legs easily and juices run clear, about 1½ hours.

Malicious Mallard

Serves 4

2 (2-pound) mallard ducks
1 tablespoon olive oil
Kosher salt and freshly ground pepper to taste
2 tablespoons herbes de Provence or a mixture of rosemary, basil,
and oregano
2 onions, sliced thick
2 cups chicken stock
1 cup red wine

Preheat the oven to 450°F.

Lightly rub ducks with olive oil and season with salt, pepper, and herbs.

Place the slices of onion on the bottom of a Dutch oven or other heavy roasting pan. Set the ducks on top. Roast in hot oven for about 30 to 45 minutes.

Pour chicken stock and red wine over ducks and cover with a tight-fitting lid or heavy-duty foil. Lower heat to 350°F and bake for an hour. Lower heat to 275°F and bake for another 2 hours, until tender and falling off the bone.

Chicken Vamp Pie

Serves 8

1 package frozen or refrigerated pie dough (should be 2 in a package)
1 egg
½ medium onion, diced
1 celery stalk, diced
1 leek, diced (white and light green parts only—discard dark green part)
2 carrots, peeled and diced
2 tablespoons butter
¼ cup all-purpose flour
3 cups chicken broth

1 large potato, peeled and cubed
1 cup cubed butternut squash
2 parsnips, diced
½ cup cut green beans
2 cups cubed cooked chicken
1 sprig thyme
1 bay leaf
½ cup frozen peas
½ cup heavy cream
Salt and pepper to taste
¼ cup chopped fresh chives

Preheat oven to 400°F. Roll out pie dough and cut into 2" circles with a round cookie cutter. You will need four circles for each serving.

For each potpie "cup" turn one ramekin upside down, oil it, and overlap four circles of pie dough around it, leaving an open hole in the bottom for juice to flow through when served. Attach dough circles to each other with egg wash (1 egg beaten with 2 tablespoons water). Bake pastry cups for about 15 minutes. Let cool and remove them from ramekins. Set aside.

Sauté onion, celery, leek, and carrots in butter until onion, celery, and leek are translucent. Dust with flour; stir and cook a few minutes. Add chicken broth, then add potato, squash, parsnips, and green beans. Add cooked chicken. Bring to a boil, add thyme and bay leaf, and simmer for 40 minutes, until the vegetables are cooked and the liquid is thickened.

Stir in peas and cream and remove from heat. Remove thyme sprig and bay leaf; season with salt and pepper. Add chives. To serve, place a pastry cup on a plate and spoon vegetables and sauce into it.

Serves 4

1 pound ground turkey
¼ cup shredded carrots
¼ cup minced onion
½ teaspoon celery salt
1 tablespoon Dijon mustard
1 tablespoon ketchup
1 teaspoon Worcestershire sauce
1 egg
1 tablespoon chopped fresh parsley
Salt and pepper
¼ cup oatmeal
¼ cup bread crumbs
3 slices bacon

Preheat oven to 350°F.

In a bowl, using your hands, combine all ingredients except for the bacon.

Shape into a loaf and press into a loaf pan.

Line the top of the meatloaf with bacon slices.

Bake until meat thermometer inserted in the center of the meatloaf reads 160°F, which should be after about 1¼ hours.

Serves 4

1½ pounds ground turkey
¼ cup sliced whole green onions
1 tablespoon Dijon mustard
1 clove garlic, minced
1 tablespoon Worcestershire sauce
½ teaspoon salt
¼ teaspoon pepper
½ cup grated Swiss cheese
¼ cup dry bread crumbs

Combine all ingredients in a bowl and mix thoroughly.

Form mixture into 4 patties, taking care not to compress them too much.

Grill or sauté burgers until cooked through, about 5 minutes per side.

TASTY TIDBIT

FANS OF TELEVISION'S *SUPERNATURAL* ARE NO STRANGERS TO THE POWER OF SALT. WHEN YOU FIND YOURSELF CORNERED IN A DARK BASEMENT WITH A DEMON HOT ON YOUR TRAIL, SIMPLY ENCIRCLE YOURSELF WITH GOOD OLD TABLE SALT AND NO HARM CAN BE DONE.

Chicken Crypt Cups
Serves 4

1 cup sliced almonds
2 boneless, skinless chicken breasts, diced
4 garlic cloves, sliced
1 teaspoon sesame oil
¼ cup sliced whole green onion
1 teaspoon cornstarch
1 tablespoon soy sauce
¼ cup hoisin sauce
1 teaspoon sugar
2 teaspoons sherry
2 tablespoons peanut oil
½ cup chicken broth
¼ cup diced fresh mushrooms
¼ cup diced canned water chestnuts
¼ cup frozen peas
8–12 lettuce cups, iceberg or butter lettuce

Preheat oven to 350°F. Lay the almonds out in an even layer on an ungreased baking sheet pan; bake for 10 minutes. Set aside.

Put chicken in a bowl with garlic, sesame oil, green onion, cornstarch, soy sauce, hoisin sauce, sugar, and sherry.

Heat wok or sauté pan and add peanut oil. Pour chicken mixture in and stir-fry for 1 minute. Add chicken broth, mushrooms, water chestnuts, and peas.

Stir-fry until chicken is cooked and sauce is thickened.

Spoon filling into lettuce cups and sprinkle with almonds. Serve immediately.

Love at First Bite

Akasha's Chicken Parmesan

Serves 4

1 cup dry bread crumbs
1 cup grated Parmesan cheese
1 tablespoon dried oregano
¼ teaspoon pepper
1 egg

½ cup flour mixed with
1 teaspoon salt
2 cups (16-oz can) tomato sauce
4 boneless, skinless chicken breasts
½ cup olive oil
4 slices mozzarella cheese

Preheat oven to 350°F. In a large bowl, combine breadcrumbs, Parmesan cheese, oregano, and pepper. In a separate bowl, beat egg with a whisk or fork. Put flour into another bowl.

Spread half of the tomato sauce on the bottom of a 9" × 13" baking dish. Dip each chicken breast first in flour, then egg, then in the bread crumb mixture.

In a large sauté pan, heat the olive oil over medium-high heat. Fry the coated chicken breasts in heated olive oil, turning when bottom side of chicken is golden brown. Place browned chicken breast slices on top of the tomato sauce in the baking dish.

Cover breasts with remaining tomato sauce. Top each breast with a slice of mozzarella and bake uncovered for 45 minutes.

TASTY TIDBIT

ACCORDING TO ANNE RICE'S VAMPIRE CHRONICLES, AKASHA AND HER HUSBAND ENKIL WERE THE VERY FIRST VAMPIRES.

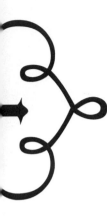

Forks Fricassee

Serves 4

1 cup all-purpose flour
1 teaspoon salt
1 teaspoon paprika
¼ teaspoon pepper
1 (3-pound) chicken, cut in 8 pieces
4 tablespoons butter
1 cup sliced onions
2 cups chicken broth
½ cup white grape juice
1 cup quartered mushrooms
1 bay leaf
½ cup heavy cream

On a dinner plate, mix together flour, salt, paprika, and pepper. Dredge chicken pieces in seasoned flour.

In a large skillet, melt butter over medium heat. Brown floured chicken pieces in butter. Remove from skillet; set aside.

Sauté the onions in the same pan, with more butter added if necessary. Pour the chicken broth and grape juice in the pan, stir, and then place the chicken back in the pan with the simmering sauce.

Add the mushrooms and the bay leaf. Cover and simmer for 45 minutes.

Take off the lid, remove the bay leaf, and stir in the heavy cream.

Simmer for 5 minutes. Serve hot.

Love at First Bite

Count Duckula's Pan-Seared Breast

Serves 2

1 boneless whole duck breast
Salt and pepper
1 shallot, chopped
1 tablespoon butter
1 fresh peach, chopped with peel on
2 tablespoons rice vinegar
1 tablespoon amaretto liqueur
½ cup chicken broth

Preheat oven to 375°F.

Score the skin on duck breast, season both sides with salt and pepper, and sear it, skin-side down, in a sauté pan over medium-high heat for 3 minutes. Remove duck breast from sauté pan and place it, skin-side up, in a baking dish. Put the duck in the oven to finish cooking for about 5 minutes.

In the same sauté pan, cook the shallots in butter for 2 minutes; add peaches, vinegar, and amaretto.

Cook to reduce liquid by half. Add broth, and cook for 5 minutes more. Adjust seasoning with salt and pepper.

Slice the duck breast and fan the slices on a plate. Spoon the peach sauce over the meat.

Deviled Smothered Cornish Hens

Serves 4

4 Cornish hens
1 cup seasoned flour
2–3 tablespoons unsalted butter
2–3 tablespoons olive oil
2 cups heavy cream
2 teaspoons dried tarragon
½ teaspoon red pepper flakes

Dredge birds in flour and sauté in melted butter and oil over medium-high heat until golden brown.

Add cream, crushed dried tarragon, and pepper flakes. Reduce heat to a simmer, cover, and cook for 1 to 1½ hours or until meat is fork tender.

TASTY TIDBIT

ELIZABETH BÁTHORY, THE BLOOD COUNTESS, BELIEVED THAT THE BLOOD OF YOUNG PEASANT GIRLS WAS THE KEY TO RETAINING HER YOUTH. SHE IS SAID TO HAVE TORTURED AND KILLED MORE THAN 500 MAIDENS IN HER LIFETIME. SUCKS TO BE HER FRIEND!

Blood Drunk Chicken Wings

Serves 4–6

8–10 chicken wings
¼ teaspoon salt
Pepper to taste
1 green onion, chopped
2 slices ginger
6 cups dry white wine to cover

In a large pot, bring 8 cups of water to a boil. While waiting for the water to boil, chop the chicken wings through the middle so that you have a drummette and the midsection. Chop off and discard the wing tips.

Cook the chicken wings in the boiling water for 5 minutes.

Add the salt, pepper, green onion, and ginger. Cover and simmer the chicken for 45 minutes. Cool.

Place the chicken wings in a sealed container and cover with the wine.

Refrigerate for at least 12 hours before serving.

Serves 4–6

4–5 pounds chicken parts
2 to 3 cups canola oil or shortening
2 eggs
2 cups milk
2½ cups all-purpose flour
1 tablespoon plus 1½ teaspoons salt, divided
2 teaspoons ground black pepper
½ teaspoon ground paprika
2 tablespoons flour
1 cup chicken broth
1 cup half-and-half or whole milk

Rinse chicken with cold water and trim excess loose skin and fat; pat dry and set aside.

Heat oil or melt shortening in a large, deep skillet with a heavy bottom and a cover. Oil is ready when it registers 350°F. Watch carefully for overheating.

Meanwhile, in a large bowl, whisk together the eggs and milk.

Combine the 2½ cups of flour, 1 tablespoon of salt, pepper, and paprika in a large food storage bag.

Dip a few chicken pieces in the milk mixture then drop in the bag and shake gently to coat thoroughly.

Working with about 4 pieces of chicken at a time, place in the hot oil. Cover and fry for 5 minutes. Uncover, fry for 5 more minutes on that side, then turn and fry the other side for about 10 minutes.

Depending on thickness and whether the meat is white or dark, the time could vary a bit. White meat generally takes less time. Check a few pieces of chicken by cutting into the meat to see if juices run clear.

Remove chicken to paper towel–lined plate to drain; sprinkle with remaining salt and keep warm. Repeat with remaining chicken pieces.

Carefully pour all but 2 tablespoons of the oil into a metal bowl or another pan; set it aside to cool before discarding.

Place the skillet with 2 tablespoons of oil over medium heat; stir in 2 tablespoons of flour, stirring up the browned bits in the bottom of the skillet.

Cook the flour and oil, stirring, for about 30 seconds. Gradually stir in the chicken broth and half-and-half.

Cook the gravy mixture, stirring constantly, until thickened and bubbly. If desired, strain before serving with the fried chicken.

Chicken with Art's Hearts

Serves 1–2

2 (5-ounce) boneless chicken thighs
⅛ teaspoon salt
⅛ teaspoon pepper
1 jar of marinated artichoke hearts
⅓ cup chicken broth
¼ cup tomato sauce
2 teaspoons granulated sugar
1 cup cooked rice or pasta

Rinse the chicken thighs and pat dry. Remove the skin and any excess fat. Rub the salt and pepper over the chicken.

Heat 2 tablespoons of the olive oil marinade from the marinated artichoke hearts in a deep-sided frying pan over medium heat. Add the chicken thighs and cook on medium heat until browned on both sides.

Drain any excess fat out of the frying pan. Add the chicken broth, tomato sauce, sugar, and the marinated artichoke hearts. Cover and simmer for 15 minutes. Make sure the chicken thighs are fully cooked through. Serve with the cooked rice or pasta.

Love at First Bite

Chicken Cacciagory

Serves 4

½ cup chopped onion
2 garlic cloves
4 chicken thighs
1 (14½-ounce) can unsalted, diced tomatoes
2 teaspoons olive oil
½ cup dry red wine
1 teaspoon dried parsley
½ teaspoon dried oregano
¼ teaspoon ground black pepper
⅛ teaspoon granulated sugar
¼ cup grated Parmesan cheese
4 cups cooked spaghetti
2 teaspoons extra-virgin olive oil

Remove the peel from the onion and chop into ¼" pieces. Peel and mince the garlic. Remove the skin from the chicken thighs. Drain the tomatoes.

Heat a deep, nonstick skillet over medium heat and add the olive oil. Add the onion and sauté until transparent. Add the garlic and chicken thighs. Sauté the chicken until lightly browned.

Remove the chicken from the pan and add the wine, tomatoes, parsley, oregano, pepper, and sugar. Stir well and bring to a boil.

Add the chicken back to the pan and sprinkle with the Parmesan cheese. Cover, reduce heat to low, and simmer for 10 minutes. Uncover and simmer for 10 more minutes.

Put 1 cup cooked pasta on each of four plates. Top each with a chicken thigh and then divide the sauce between the dishes. Drizzle ½ teaspoon olive oil over the top of each dish.

Haunted Jungle Chicken

Serves 2–3

2–4 serrano peppers, stems and seeds removed
1 stalk lemongrass, inner portion roughly chopped
2 (2"-long, ½"-wide) strips of lime peel
2 tablespoons vegetable oil
½ cup coconut milk
1 whole boneless, skinless chicken breast, cut into thin strips
2–4 tablespoons fish sauce
10–15 basil leaves

Place the peppers, lemongrass, and lime peel into a food processor and process until ground.

Heat the oil over medium-high heat in a wok or large skillet. Add the pepper mixture and sauté for 1 to 2 minutes.

Stir in the coconut milk and cook for 2 minutes.

Add the chicken and cook until the chicken is cooked through, about 5 minutes.

Reduce heat to low and add the fish sauce and basil leaves to taste.

Serve with plenty of jasmine rice.

Chicken of the Midnight King

Serves 4

1 can cream of chicken soup
¼ cup skim milk
½ teaspoon Worcestershire sauce
1 tablespoon mayonnaise
¼ teaspoon ground black pepper
2 cups frozen mix of peas and pearl onions, thawed
1 cup frozen sliced carrots, thawed
1 cup sliced mushrooms, steamed
½ pound (8 ounces) cooked, chopped chicken
4 slices whole-wheat bread, toasted

Combine the soup, milk, Worcestershire, mayonnaise, and pepper in a saucepan and bring to a boil.

Reduce heat and add the peas and pearl onions, carrots, mushrooms, and chicken.

Simmer until the vegetables and chicken are heated through. Serve over toast.

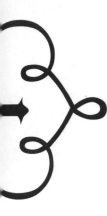

Tortellini by Twilight with Pesto Chicken
Serves 6

1 (9-ounce) package refrigerated cheese tortellini
2 tablespoons butter
2 tablespoons olive oil
1 onion, chopped
4 boneless, skinless chicken breasts, cut into 2" cubes
1 (16-ounce) jar four-cheese Alfredo sauce
½ cup basil pesto
½ cup grated Parmesan cheese

Bring a large pot of salted water to a boil and add the tortellini. Cook according to package directions, then drain well and set aside.

Meanwhile, in large skillet, heat butter and olive oil over medium heat. Add onion and chicken breasts; cook and stir until chicken is almost cooked through but still pink in the center, about 5 to 7 minutes.

Add Alfredo sauce to skillet and bring to a simmer. Add cooked and drained tortellini; simmer for 2 to 4 minutes longer, until chicken is thoroughly cooked. Stir in pesto and cheese and serve.

Chicken Cordon Black and Bleu

Serves 4

1 cup grated Parmesan cheese
4 boneless, skinless chicken breasts
8 slices pancetta
1 14-ounce jar Alfredo sauce
4 slices baby Swiss cheese

Preheat oven to 400°F. Place ½ cup Parmesan cheese on a plate and dip chicken breasts into cheese to coat. Wrap pancetta around chicken breasts and place in a 2-quart casserole dish. Bake for 10 minutes. In medium bowl, combine Alfredo sauce with remaining ½ cup Parmesan cheese.

Remove casserole from oven and pour Alfredo sauce mixture over chicken. Return to oven and bake for 10 minutes longer. Top each chicken breast with a slice of cheese and return to oven. Bake for 5 minutes longer or until chicken is thoroughly cooked and cheese is melted.

Chicken Victoria

Serves 4

¼ cup flour
½ teaspoon salt
⅛ teaspoon pepper
½ teaspoon dried marjoram leaves
4 boneless, skinless chicken breasts
¼ cup butter
1 cup chicken stock
½ cup white grape juice
1 cup red grapes, cut in half

On a shallow plate, combine flour, salt, pepper, and marjoram. Coat chicken breasts in this mixture. In a heavy skillet over medium heat, melt butter. Add chicken breasts and cook for 4 minutes. Turn chicken over and cook 3 to 6 minutes longer, until chicken is just done. Remove chicken from pan and cover with foil to keep warm.

Add stock and grape juice to pan and bring to a boil, scraping up pan drippings. Boil over high heat for 6 to 8 minutes, until sauce is reduced and thickened. Return chicken to pan along with red grapes, and cook over low heat for 2 to 3 minutes, until grapes are hot and chicken is tender.

Love at First Bite

Louisiana Bat Wings

Serves 8

1 small onion
1 jalapeño pepper
1 cup Louisiana red pepper sauce
2 tablespoons Worcestershire sauce
1 tablespoons powdered Cajun spice, divided
1 cup barbecue sauce
5 pounds thawed chicken wings, disjointed with tips removed

Preheat slow cooker on high setting. Peel the onion and chop it into ¼" pieces. Remove and discard the stem and seeds from the jalapeño pepper; dice the pepper.

Add the onion, jalapeño pepper, red pepper sauce, Worcestershire sauce, Cajun spice, and barbecue sauce to the slow cooker and stir well.

Add the chicken wings and stir until all the wings are covered.

Cover and cook on high setting for 4 hours. Uncover and turn heat to low while serving.

Turkey Armandine

Serves 4

2 tablespoons olive oil
1 cup sliced carrots
2 cups shredded cooked turkey
1 (14-ounce) jar turkey gravy
½ cup whipping cream
½ cup toasted sliced almonds

In a saucepan, heat olive oil over medium heat. Add carrots; cook and stir until crisp-tender, about 4 to 5 minutes. Add shredded turkey and stir.

Add gravy and whipping cream and bring to a simmer. Cook for 3 to 5 minutes, until turkey and carrots are hot and tender.

Sprinkle with almonds and serve.

TASTY TIDBIT

In *Interview with the Vampire*, Armand is the 400-year-old vampire that runs the Theatre des Vampires. Louis is intrigued by his new vampire friends but he learns quickly they are not to be trusted.

Deadly Divan

Serves 4–6

1 package frozen broccoli florets
4 large boneless, skinless chicken breasts, cooked and diced
2 cans cream of chicken soup
1 cup mayonnaise
1 (8-ounce) package shredded Cheddar cheese
2 cups stuffing mix

———

Place frozen broccoli in a well-buttered casserole dish.

Top with diced chicken.

Combine cream of chicken soup, mayonnaise, and Cheddar cheese and spread over chicken.

Sprinkle stuffing mix on top and bake at 325°F for 30 minutes.

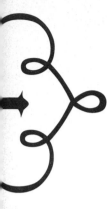

Toothsome Turkey Tenderloin with Lime

Serves 4

1 tablespoon olive oil
2 shallots, minced
1 turkey tenderloin, cubed
½ teaspoon salt
⅛ teaspoon white pepper
2 tablespoons flour
½ teaspoon dried thyme leaves
3 tablespoons lime juice
1 cup apple juice
2 tablespoons cornstarch
½ cup chicken or beef broth

Heat olive oil in large skillet over medium heat. Cook shallots for 2 to 3 minutes, stirring frequently. Sprinkle turkey with salt, pepper, and flour. Add turkey to skillet and cook, turning to brown evenly, until tender and juices run clear when a piece is pierced, about 8 to 10 minutes.

In a small bowl combine thyme, lime juice, apple juice, cornstarch, and broth. Add to skillet; cook and stir over medium heat until thickened and bubbly, about 3 to 4 minutes. Serve immediately.

Love at First Bite

CHAPTER 7

MURDEROUS MEATS

*Flesh and Bones to
Sink Your Teeth Into*

Blood Dripping Tri-Tip
Serves 6

1 tablespoon freshly cracked peppercorns
2 teaspoons garlic salt
1 teaspoon dry mustard
¼ teaspoon cayenne pepper
2–3 pound tri-tip roast
Oak, mesquite, or hickory chips for grilling

Mix together the peppercorns, garlic salt, mustard, and cayenne. Rub into the surface of the tri-tip. Cover with plastic wrap and refrigerate overnight.

Soak the wood chips in water for at least 30 minutes. Preheat grill to medium. Add the soaked woods chips to the coals.

Sear the tri-tip directly over medium heat, turning once, to seal in juices, about 2 minutes on each side. Then grill the tri-tip indirectly over medium heat, turning once, until the internal temperature is about 140°F. Grill an additional 30 minutes.

Remove from heat and let stand for 5 minutes. Slice diagonally against the grain.

TASTY TIDBIT

Try pairing this dish with Great Lakes Brewing Company's handcrafted Nosferatu Ale. It's a seasonal offering, so look for it in early Fall.

Love at First Bite

Steak Through the Heart

Serves 2–4

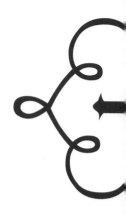

12 ounces beef round steak
2 tablespoons soy sauce
1 teaspoon cornstarch
1 green bell pepper
¼ cup chopped onion
1 garlic clove
2 tablespoons olive oil
½ cup crushed tomatoes
½ cup water
1 teaspoon granulated sugar
¼ teaspoon celery salt

Cut the beef across the grain into thin strips about 2" long. Place the beef in a bowl. Add 1 tablespoon of the soy sauce and the cornstarch to the beef, mixing the cornstarch into the meat with your fingers. Let marinate for 20 to 30 minutes.

While the beef is marinating, prepare the vegetables. Wash the pepper, remove the seeds, and cut into cubes. Smash, peel, and chop the garlic clove.

Heat 1 tablespoon olive oil in a frying pan. Add the meat. Cook until browned on both sides. Remove and set aside.

Clean out the pan and add 1 tablespoon olive oil. Add the chopped onion and garlic clove. Cook on medium heat until the onion is tender. Add the crushed tomatoes, pepper, water, sugar, celery salt, and the remaining 1 tablespoon soy sauce. Bring to a boil, reduce heat to medium-low, and cook for 5 minutes.

Return the meat to the pan. Cover and simmer for 45 minutes or until the meat is tender. Serve hot with brown rice.

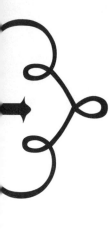

Stoker's Stroganoff
Serves 4

16 ounces egg noodles
2 tablespoons butter or margarine
½ red onion, chopped
1 cup canned sliced mushrooms, drained
1¼ pounds ground beef
⅛ teaspoon (or to taste) salt
⅛ teaspoon (or to taste) black pepper
½ teaspoon (or to taste) dried parsley flakes
½ cup beef broth
¼ cup (or to taste) sour cream

Cook the egg noodles according to the package directions. Drain and set aside.

Melt the butter or margarine in a frying pan over medium heat. Add the chopped onion and the mushrooms. Sauté until the onion is tender. Remove the onion and mushrooms from the pan.

Add the ground beef to the pan. Cook on medium heat until browned. Drain off any excess fat. Stir in the salt, pepper, and dried parsley.

Add the onion and mushrooms back to the pan. Add the beef broth. Heat through, and stir in the sour cream. Heat for a few more minutes, and serve over the noodles.

Love at First Bite

Suicidal Swine

Serves 2–4

1 pound lean boneless pork
½ large green or red bell pepper
¼ cup baby carrots
1 green onion, (optional)
⅓ cup white vinegar
2 tablespoons ketchup
3 tablespoons granulated sugar
⅓ cup plus 2 tablespoons water
2 tablespoons vegetable oil
1 tablespoon cornstarch

Cut the pork into cubes. Wash and drain all the vegetables. Cut the bell pepper into cubes, and cut the baby carrots in half. Dice the green onion, if using.

In a small bowl, combine the vinegar, ketchup, sugar, and ⅓ cup water, and set aside.

Heat the oil in a frying pan on medium to medium-high heat. When the oil is hot, add the pork cubes and brown. Drain off the fat from the pan and add the sauce. Reduce heat to medium-low, cover, and simmer for 45 minutes or until tender.

Combine the cornstarch and 2 tablespoons water in a small bowl. Increase heat to high and add the cornstarch mixture, stirring to thicken. Reduce heat to medium and add the green pepper and carrots. Cover and simmer for 10 minutes or until the vegetables are tender. Stir in the green onion if using. Serve hot over rice.

Kappa Kielbasa

Yields 1½ pounds

1 pound (16 ounces) pork shoulder
½ pound beef chuck
2 teaspoons minced garlic
1 tablespoon brown sugar
1 teaspoon freshly ground black pepper
½ teaspoon ground allspice
1 teaspoon fresh marjoram
Sea or kosher salt

Remove all fat from the meat. Cut the meat into cubes, put them in a food processor, and grind to desired consistency.

Add the remaining ingredients and mix until well blended. You can put the sausage mixture in casings, but it works equally well broiled or grilled as patties.

TASTY TIDBIT

A KAPPA IS A CREEPY CRITTER RESEMBLING A HAIRLESS MONKEY WITH LARGE ROUND EYES AND WEBBED FINGERS AND TOES. IT SPRINGS FROM ITS HIDING PLACES IN WATERWAYS AND PONDS, AND HAS THE DISTASTEFUL HABIT OF SUCKING BLOOD FROM ITS VICTIMS THROUGH THEIR INTESTINES.

Love at First Bite

Bram's Bolognese

Serves 4

½ large onion, chopped
2 cloves garlic, minced
2 tablespoons olive oil
1 pound ground beef
1 (28-ounce) can crushed tomatoes
1 teaspoon dried oregano
1 teaspoon dried basil
1 teaspoon salt
½ teaspoon pepper

Sauté onions and garlic in olive oil until soft.

Add ground beef to the pan and cook, stirring occasionally, until brown.

Pour in the crushed tomatoes and bring to a simmer.

Stir in the herbs, salt, and pepper, and then simmer uncovered for an hour.

Adjust seasoning with salt and pepper.

Black-Magic Steak

Serves 2

2 ½ pound filets (or any cut of your choosing), ½" to ¾" thick
⅓ cup melted butter
Chef Paul Prudhomme's Blackened Steak Magic Blend

Preheat a cast-iron skillet for at least 10 minutes. The hotter the pan, the better.

Coat both sides of steak in melted butter.

Sprinkle Blackened Steak Magic Blend on both sides of the meat and rub into the meat. The more you sprinkle and rub, the more intense the flavor.

Cook steak over high heat until the underside forms a slight crust (about 30 seconds). Flip and repeat. Be careful not to burn the meat. Serve hot and juicy.

TASTY TIDBIT

CURIOUSLY, SOME LEGENDS MAKE MENTION THAT A STAKE IS ONLY TO BE HAMMERED INTO THE CHEST IN ONE BLOW, FOR IF IT'S STRUCK TWICE, THE REVENANT CAN REANIMATE AND RETURN TO ITS VAMPIRIC STATE.

Bloody Joes

Serves 6–8

2 teaspoons butter or margarine
1 yellow onion, chopped
2 red bell peppers, sliced
2 pounds ground beef
2 cups canned kidney beans
2 cups tomato sauce
4 tablespoons tomato paste
1 cup water
1 teaspoon ground cumin
2 teaspoons granulated sugar
6–8 hamburger buns

Heat the butter or margarine on medium in a large frying pan or saucepan. Add the onion. Cook for 1 minute, then add the bell peppers.

Add the ground beef. Cook over medium heat until browned. Drain off any excess fat.

Add the kidney beans, tomato sauce, tomato paste, and water. Mix thoroughly and stir in the ground cumin and sugar.

Bring to a boil. Cover and simmer for 20 to 25 minutes, until heated thoroughly. Spoon the meat mixture over the hamburger buns, or serve in a large pot and invite guests to prepare their own.

Evil Eye Steaks with Onions

Serves 4

4 large white onions
4 garlic cloves
2 tablespoons olive oil
4 boneless rib-eye steaks, 1" thick
½ teaspoon salt
½ teaspoon ground black pepper
4 teaspoons dry vermouth

Peel and slice the onions. Peel the garlic cloves and split in half.

In a large skillet, heat the olive oil on medium; cook the onions in the oil until golden brown, about 10 to 15 minutes. Cover and keep warm.

Rub both sides of the steaks with the cut-side of the garlic and season with salt and pepper. Grill the steaks for 3 to 4 minutes on each side, or to the desired degree of doneness.

Pour 1 teaspoon vermouth over each steak immediately before removing from the grill. Serve with grilled onions.

Love at First Bite

Fang Banger Ribs
Serves 4

3 pounds baby back ribs
1 (32-ounce) container sauerkraut
3 cups shredded red cabbage
4 garlic cloves
1 (14½-ounce) can stewed tomatoes
2 tablespoons plus 1 teaspoon paprika
1 teaspoon salt
1 teaspoon ground black pepper

Trim the ribs of excess fat. Drain and rinse the sauerkraut. Shred the red cabbage. Peel and mince the garlic.

Preheat oven to 375°F.

In a medium-sized bowl, combine the sauerkraut, cabbage, garlic, tomatoes, and 1 teaspoon of the paprika; stir well to mix. Spread this mixture into the bottom of a large, oiled baking dish.

Arrange the ribs on top of the sauerkraut mixture, curved side up. Season with salt and pepper and the rest of the paprika. Bake in the oven, covered, for about 1 to 1½ hours or until the meat is tender. Uncover the pan, turn the ribs over, and bake uncovered for another 20 minutes. To serve, cut the ribs apart from the bones and serve over the sauerkraut.

Lilith's London Broil

Serves 4

5 garlic cloves
1 green onion
½ cup dry red wine
¼ cup olive oil
2 tablespoons red wine vinegar
1¼ teaspoon Worcestershire sauce

2-pound London broil
1 teaspoon salt
1 teaspoon ground black pepper
1 tablespoon butter
1 pound fresh mushrooms

Peel and mince 2 of the garlic cloves. Peel and sliver the remaining 3 garlic cloves. Keep separate. Finely chop the green onion.

In a small mixing bowl, combine the minced garlic, green onion, red wine, oil, vinegar, and Worcestershire sauce.

Poke several small holes in the London Broil and place the garlic slivers in the holes. Place the meat in a shallow baking pan and pour the wine mixture over the meat. Cover and refrigerate for several hours.

Preheat grill to medium-high. Grill the London broil for 3 minutes. Turn and sprinkle the cooked side with salt and pepper. Cook for another 3 minutes or until cooked to your liking.

Sauté the sliced mushrooms in butter and serve over cooked meat.

TASTY TIDBIT

ACCORDING TO HEBREW BELIEF, LILITH WAS ADAM'S FIRST WIFE—NOT EVE. AFTER LEAVING THE GARDEN OF EDEN, SHE CONSORTED WITH DEMONS AND CREATED AN ENTIRE RACE OF FEMALE VAMPIRES CALLED LAMIAS. SHE IS CONSIDERED TO BE ONE OF THE EARLIEST VAMPIRE FIGURES.

Love at First Bite

Claudia's Corned Beef and Cabbage

Serves 6

3-pound corned beef brisket

6 medium carrots

3 medium potatoes

3 medium parsnips

6 small yellow onions

½ medium head cabbage

1½ teaspoons whole black peppercorns

2 bay leaves

1½ cups milk

4 teaspoons cornstarch

2 tablespoons horseradish mustard

Trim excess fat from the meat. Peel the carrots, potatoes, and parsnips and cut into chunks. Peel the onions and cut in half. Shred the cabbage.

Place the meat in a Dutch oven. Add enough water to cover the meat. Add the peppercorns and bay leaves. Bring to a boil. Reduce heat and simmer, covered, for 2 hours.

Add the vegetables to the Dutch oven. Reduce heat, cook until the vegetables are tender.

Remove the meat and vegetables from the liquid. Discard the liquid and bay leaves. Slice the meat across the grain.

Make the mustard sauce by stirring together the milk and cornstarch in a small saucepan. Cook and stir until thickened and bubbly. Stir in the mustard. Heat through.

Put the meat and vegetables on a platter and drizzle with the sauce.

TASTY TIDBIT

KIRSTEN DUNST PORTRAYED THIS GOLDEN-HAIRED CHILD VAMPIRE IN *INTERVIEW WITH THE VAMPIRE*. LUCKY GIRL EVEN GOT TO LOCK LIPS WITH BRAD PITT!

The Hunter's Ham
Serves 12

4-pound boneless ham
30 whole cloves
3 tablespoons chutney of your choice
1 packed tablespoon dark brown sugar
2 tablespoons prepared horseradish mustard
2 teaspoons fresh rosemary leaves

Preheat oven to 325°F. Place the ham in a roasting pan set on a rack. Insert the whole cloves all over the ham and bake for about 1½ hours or until the internal temperature reads 130°F.

Meanwhile, in a small saucepan, combine the chutney, brown sugar, mustard, and rosemary. Cook over low heat until warm and liquefied.

Drizzle the glaze over the ham and bake for an additional 30 minutes or until the internal temperature reads 140°F. The outside of the ham should be crusty and sugary brown.

TASTY TIDBIT

A VAMPIRE HUNTER SHOULD NEVER LEAVE HOME WITHOUT THE FOLLOWING ITEMS: STAKES, CRUCIFIXES, HOLY WATER, MIRRORS, GARLIC, AND A BIBLE. THESE CAN ALL BE SAFELY STORED IN A WOODEN BOX, PREFERABLY MADE OF ASH OR HAWTHORN. BE SURE TO CARVE A CROSS ON THE TOP TO DISSUADE INQUISITIVE VAMPIRES FROM SNOOPING INSIDE.

Love at First Bite

Spooktacular Shepherd's Pie

Serves 4

1 small onion, diced
1 pound ground beef
1 can of beef gravy
Salt and pepper to taste
1 package of frozen corn niblets
3 cups mashed potatoes
1 can of French fried onions

Preheat oven to 400°F.

Sauté onion in a large frying pan. When the onion is translucent, add the beef and cook until browned.

Drain excess fat from beef and add can of beef gravy. Simmer until the mixture is thickened, season with salt and pepper.

Place a layer of corn on the bottom of an ungreased 9" × 13" casserole dish. Pour beef mixture over the corn.

Spread mashed potatoes over the meat mixture, and cover the top with French fried onions.

Bake for 20 minutes.

Lustful Loin

Serves 4

1 garlic clove
1 teaspoon olive oil
1 teaspoon brown sugar
¼ teaspoon dried thyme
¼ teaspoon dried sage
¼ teaspoon freshly ground black pepper
½ pound boneless pork loin roast
¼ cup chopped or ground pecans

Crush the garlic with the side of a large knife. Remove the skin. Put the olive oil, garlic, brown sugar, and seasonings in a resealable plastic bag. Mix well. Add the roast and turn it in the bag to coat the meat. Marinate in the refrigerator for 6 to 12 hours.

Preheat oven to 400°F.

Roll the pork loin in the chopped pecans and place in a roasting pan. Make a tent of aluminum foil and arrange it over the pork loin, covering the nuts completely so that they won't burn. Roast for 10 minutes, then lower the heat to 350°F. Continue to roast for an additional 8 to 15 minutes or until the meat thermometer reads 150°F to 170°F, depending on how well done you prefer it. Let sit for 10 minutes before serving.

Serves 4

4 teaspoons soy sauce
4 teaspoons burgundy wine
2 teaspoons brown sugar
¼ teaspoon honey
¼ teaspoon garlic powder
¼ teaspoon ground cinnamon
4 (8-ounce) pork tenderloins

Combine the soy sauce, burgundy wine, brown sugar, honey, garlic powder, and ground cinnamon in a resealable plastic bag; shake well. Add the tenderloins and shake gently until the meat is well coated. Place in the refrigerator for at least 1 hour.

Heat coals or gas grill until moderately hot. Grill the tenderloins on both sides until meat thermometer hits 160°F. Allow the meat to rest for 10 minutes in its juices. Slice and serve.

Lestat's Leg of Lamb

Serves 12

4-pound leg of lamb
2 (12-ounce) cans beer (ale)
3 bay leaves
¼ bunch parsley, chopped
4 sprigs thyme, chopped
3 sprigs mint, chopped
Fresh-cracked black pepper, to taste

Kosher salt, to taste
1 cup beef stock
4 yellow onions
2 stalks celery
2 carrots
6 cloves garlic

Marinate the lamb overnight in a mixture of the beer, herbs, and spices.

Preheat oven to 325°F.

Remove the lamb from the marinade. Heat large roasting pan on stovetop and sear lamb quickly on all sides, add stock, cover, and braise for 3 hours.

While the lamb cooks, chop the onions, celery, and carrots. Peel the garlic and leave the cloves whole. Place the vegetables and garlic in the bottom of another roasting pan; roast for approximately 30 minutes, until tender.

Preheat grill. Remove the lamb from oven and discard the liquid. Place the lamb on the grill to brown on all sides, then serve with the vegetables.

TASTY TIDBIT

IT'S SAID THAT LESTAT WAS BASED ON BOTH RICE AND HER HUSBAND, STAN. IN LIFE, LESTAT WAS FROM AN ARISTOCRATIC LINEAGE FALLEN ON HARD TIMES DURING THE 1780S. BORN AS A VAMPIRE BY MAGNUS IN THE LATTER PART OF THE 1700S, LESTAT IS, IN ALL HIS VANITY AND BOLD ENDEAVORS, THE QUINTESSENTIAL VAMPIRE OF THE MODERN ERA.

Stuffed Skull Tops

Serves 4

4 green peppers
1 pound ground beef
¼ pound ground pork
½ cup white long-grain rice, uncooked
½ cup diced onion
1 (16-ounce) can tomato sauce

Preheat oven to 350°F.

Cut peppers in half through the stem and discard seeds, stem, and membrane. Lay pepper cups in an ungreased 9" × 13" casserole dish.

In a bowl mix together the meat, rice, onion, and ½ cup tomato sauce. Season mixture with a bit of salt and pepper.

Stuff each pepper half with a ball of meat mixture, mounding it on top.

Pour tomato sauce over tops of stuffed peppers, cover with foil, and bake 45 minutes to 1 hour.

Pandora's Pot Roast

Serves 4

1 large onion
1- to 2-pound beef roast
3 carrots, peeled
2 celery stalks
2 large potatoes, peeled
1 cup beef broth
½ teaspoon salt
¼ teaspoon pepper
1 tablespoon chopped parsley

Preheat oven to 325°F.

Cut onion into large chunks and scatter them on the bottom of a roasting pan.

Put the meat on top of the onions.

Cut the carrots, celery, and potatoes into 2" chunks and scatter them around the meat. Pour the broth over the meat. Sprinkle the salt, pepper, and parsley over the meat and vegetables.

Cover and roast in the oven for 2 to 2½ hours.

TASTY TIDBIT

ANOTHER ANNE RICE CREATION, PANDORA IS AN ANCIENT VAMPIRE AND WAS THERE DURING AKASHA'S KILLING SPREE IN *THE QUEEN OF THE DAMNED*. RICE'S BOOK *PANDORA* WAS PUBLISHED IN 1998.

Sticky Ribs
Serves 2

2 tablespoons paprika
1 clove garlic, minced
2 teaspoons salt
1 teaspoon sugar
1 teaspoon pepper
1 teaspoon dried oregano
1 teaspoon dried thyme
1 slab baby back pork ribs
½ cup barbecue sauce

Preheat oven to 350°F.

Mix dry ingredients together in a bowl, and then rub the mixture on both sides of the ribs.

Place ribs in a roasting pan, cover, and bake for 2 hours.

Remove cooked ribs from oven. Brush on barbecue sauce, and bake uncovered for 10 minutes.

Cut slab in half to serve two.

Lamia's Lamb Chops

Serves 4

1½ cups dry bread crumbs
1 tablespoon chopped fresh rosemary
4 basil leaves, minced
2 tablespoons olive oil
12 lamb chops
Salt and pepper, to taste
4 tablespoons butter

Combine bread crumbs, herbs, and olive oil. Set aside.

Season lamb chops with salt and pepper. Sauté them in butter until medium-rare; transfer to a broiler pan. Heat the broiler.

Mound 2 tablespoons of bread-crumb mixture on each lamb chop.

Broil chops until crust is sufficiently browned.

TASTY TIDBIT

THE WRITINGS AND LEGENDS OF ANCIENT GREEKS TELL THE TALE OF AN ILLICIT LOVE AFFAIR BETWEEN THE OMNIPOTENT ZEUS AND THE LIBYAN PRINCESS LAMIA. THE DOWNSIDE OF THIS CELESTIAL FLING IS THAT IT ATTRACTED THE WRATH OF HERA, ZEUS'S JEALOUS WIFE, WHO TOOK VENGEANCE UPON LAMIA BY KILLING ALL OF HER GOD-SPAWNED CHILDREN. GRIEF-STRICKEN, LAMIA STRUCK HER REVENGE UPON HUMANKIND BY STEALING AND SUCKING THE LIFE FROM THE BABIES OF MORTAL MOTHERS.

Fangtasia Fiesta Casserole
Serves 4–6

1 (18-ounce) package cooked ground beef in taco sauce
1½ cups frozen corn
1 (15-ounce) can dark kidney beans, rinsed and drained
1 (8-ounce) package tortilla chips
1½ cups shredded Cheddar cheese
½ cup shredded pepper jack cheese

Preheat oven to 400°F. In large skillet, combine ground beef, corn, and kidney beans over medium heat. Cook, stirring occasionally, until mixture comes to a boil; reduce heat and simmer for 5 minutes.

In 2-quart casserole, layer a third of the beef mixture, a third of the chips, and a third of the cheeses. Repeat layers, ending with cheeses. Bake for 20 to 30 minutes, until hot and bubbly. Serve with sour cream, shredded lettuce, avocados, and more shredded cheese.

TASTY TIDBIT

WHETHER FOR HALLOWEEN OR ANY DAY OF THE YEAR, IF YOU NEED A PAIR OF CUSTOMIZED FANGS TO COMPLETE YOUR GOTHIC GET-UP CHECK OUT THIS SITE: *WWW.VAMPFANGS.COM.*

Stalker's Steak Stir-Fry
Serves 4

1 pound sirloin steak
½ teaspoon salt
⅛ teaspoon pepper
3 tablespoons butter
1 tablespoon olive oil
1 onion, thinly sliced
3 cloves garlic, minced
1 (8-ounce) package sliced button mushrooms
2 (5-ounce) packages prepared fresh green beans
2 tablespoons Worcestershire sauce
½ teaspoon dry mustard powder
2 tablespoons lemon juice
1 cup beef broth
2 tablespoons cornstarch
2 tablespoons chopped fresh parsley

Trim excess fat from steak, cut in half, and cut across the grain (or perpendicular to the lines in the meat) into ½" strips. Sprinkle with salt and pepper. In heavy skillet, melt butter and olive oil; add the steak strips and stir-fry until brown, about 3 to 4 minutes. Remove meat from skillet to a plate with slotted spoon.

To drippings remaining in skillet, add onion and garlic; stir-fry until crisp-tender, about 3 to 4 minutes. Add mushrooms and green beans; stir-fry for 3 to 5 minutes longer. Add Worcestershire sauce, mustard powder, lemon juice, beef broth, and cornstarch, and bring to a simmer.

Return meat to skillet; bring back to a simmer and cook for 4 to 5 minutes longer, until meat and vegetables are tender. Sprinkle with parsley and serve.

Love at First Bite

Naughty Brats

Serves 6–8

8 bratwursts
2 onions, sliced
4 cloves garlic, sliced
1 (12-ounce) can beer
½ cup water
Hot dog buns

Place bratwursts in heavy skillet over medium-high heat. Cook bratwursts, turning with tongs, until browned on all sides, about 8 to 9 minutes total. Remove to 4-quart slow cooker. In drippings remaining in skillet, cook onion until crisp-tender, about 4 minutes. Add to slow cooker along with garlic, beer, and water. Cover and cook on high for 4 to 5 hours, until bratwursts are thoroughly cooked.

You can turn the slow cooker to low and let the brats sit for up to 2 hours. When ready to serve, remove brats with tongs and remove onions and garlic with a slotted spoon. Serve brats on buns with the onions and garlic, lots of grainy mustard, and cold beer.

Creepy Crepes

Serves 4–6

2 tablespoons butter
1 green bell pepper, chopped
3 cloves garlic, minced
2 shallots, minced
2 cups cubed ham
1 (16-ounce) jar Alfredo sauce
1 cup shredded Gruyère cheese
16 crepes
⅓ cup grated Parmesan cheese
1 teaspoon paprika

In medium microwave-safe bowl, combine butter, bell pepper, garlic, and shallots. Microwave on high for 1 minute, remove and stir, then return to microwave oven and cook on high for 1 minute longer. Remove and stir in ham and 1 cup of the Alfredo sauce. Stir in the Gruyère cheese.

Place crepes on work surface and divide ham mixture among them. Roll up, enclosing filling. Pour half of remaining Alfredo sauce into bottom of 3-quart shallow microwave-safe baking dish. Arrange filled crepes over sauce. Spoon remaining sauce over crepes and sprinkle with Parmesan cheese and paprika. Microwave on 70 percent power for 5 minutes, then turn dish and microwave on 70 percent power for 3 to 6 minutes longer, until crepes are hot. Remove from microwave and let stand on solid surface for 5 minutes, then serve.

Pork du Pointe du Lac

Serves 4

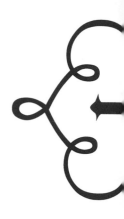

¾ pound pork tenderloin
1 tablespoon soy sauce
1 tablespoon apple juice
1½ teaspoons cornstarch
1 tablespoon water
2 tablespoons plus 1 teaspoon vegetable oil
1 teaspoon minced ginger
2 teaspoons curry powder
2 large peaches, thinly sliced
½ cup chicken broth
Black pepper, to taste

Cut the pork into 1" cubes. Place the pork in a medium bowl and toss with the soy sauce and apple juice. Let stand for 5 minutes.

In a small bowl, dissolve the cornstarch in the water.

Heat 2 tablespoons oil in a skillet on medium-high heat. Add the pork and half the ginger. Cook, stirring constantly, until the pork is no longer pink and is nearly cooked through.

Push the pork to the sides of the pan. Add 1 teaspoon oil in the middle. Add the remainder of the ginger and the curry powder. Stir for a few seconds until aromatic. Add the sliced peaches. Cook for a minute, stirring continually, and add the chicken broth. Add the cornstarch and water mixture, stirring to thicken.

Season with the pepper. Cook for another minute, stirring to mix everything together. Serve hot.

Ghastly Ghoulash

Serves 6

2 pounds beef round steak
3 tablespoons flour
1 teaspoon salt
⅛ teaspoon pepper
1 tablespoon sweet paprika
2 tablespoons olive oil
1 onion, chopped
3 russet potatoes, chopped
½ cup water
2 (8-ounce) cans tomato sauce with roasted garlic
1 cup sour cream

Cut steak into 1" pieces. In small bowl, combine flour, salt, pepper, and paprika. Sprinkle over beef cubes and rub into meat. Heat olive oil in pressure cooker; add beef and brown on all sides, stirring frequently, about 3 to 5 minutes. Meanwhile, prepare the onions and potatoes.

Add onion and potatoes to pressure cooker along with water and tomato sauce. Lock the lid and bring up to high pressure. Cook for 12 minutes, then release pressure using quick-release method. Test to be sure potatoes are tender; if not, lock lid and cook for 2 to 3 minutes longer. Then release pressure, stir in sour cream, and serve over hot cooked buttered noodles or mashed potatoes.

Merlotte's Mini Meatloaf

Serves 6

2 eggs
½ teaspoon dried Italian seasoning
½ teaspoon onion salt
⅛ teaspoon garlic pepper
¾ cup soft bread crumbs
¾ cup ketchup
1½ pounds meatloaf mix
1 cup shredded Colby jack cheese

Preheat oven to 350°F. In large bowl, combine eggs, Italian seasoning, onion salt, garlic pepper, bread crumbs, and ½ cup ketchup and mix well. Add meatloaf mix and ½ cup cheese and mix gently but thoroughly to combine.

Press meat mixture, ⅓ cup at a time, into 12 muffin cups. Top each with a bit of ketchup and remaining cheese. Bake at 350°F for 15 to 18 minutes, until meat is thoroughly cooked. Remove from muffin tins, drain if necessary, place on serving platter, cover with foil, and let stand for 5 minutes before serving.

TASTY TIDBIT

MERLOTTE'S IS THE LOCAL BAR AND GRILL WHERE SOOKIE STACKHOUSE WAITS TABLES AND SERVES UP PLENTY OF TRUE BLOOD TO THE LOCAL VAMPS.

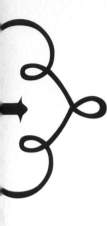

Caustic Veal Meatballs
Serves 4

1 pound ground veal
1 teaspoon salt
1 teaspoon pepper
1 teaspoon garlic powder
2 tablespoons canola oil
1 green bell pepper, cut into ¼" cubes
1 medium onion, chopped
2 large carrots, grated
2 tablespoons vinegar
3 tablespoons brown sugar
2 teaspoons reduced-sodium soy sauce
2 teaspoons dry sherry
2 tablespoons cornstarch
½ cup chilled chicken broth

Mix together veal, salt, pepper, and garlic powder in a medium bowl.

Roll veal mixture into 1" meatballs.

Heat oil in a large skillet, over low heat. Brown the meatballs on all sides, approximately 3 to 5 minutes.

Add bell pepper, onion, carrots, vinegar, brown sugar, soy sauce, and sherry. Cover and simmer, stirring constantly.

Mix cornstarch and chicken broth in a small bowl. Add to skillet.

Wait for mixture to thicken, and cook 5 to 10 more minutes. Serve immediately, perhaps over brown rice.

Love at First Bite

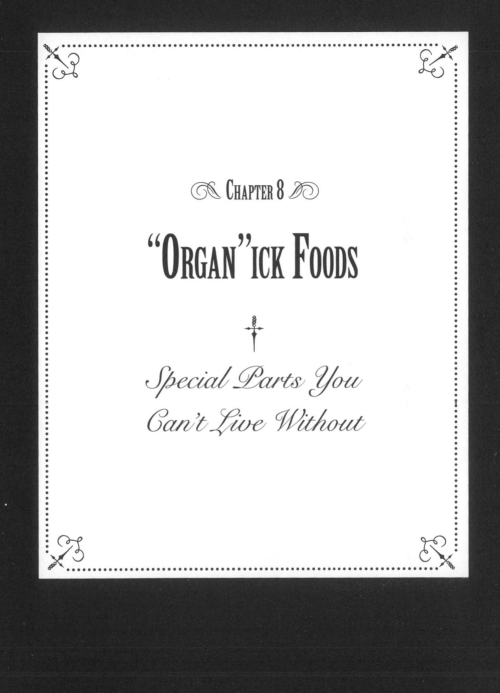

CHAPTER 8

"Organ"ick Foods

Special Parts You
Can't Live Without

Serves 4

1½ pounds liver (any type)
8 strips bacon
2 onions, sliced

Slice liver very thin. Keep refrigerated until ready to use.

Fry bacon until crispy and brown. Set aside.

Sauté onions in bacon grease until wilted and slightly browned. Remove with a slotted spoon and drain on paper towels.

Sauté liver slices over high heat, searing for about a minute or less on each side.

Serve liver topped with onion and 2 slices of bacon per serving.

TASTY TIDBIT

A unique addition to Bulgarian vampire lore is the *ustrel*, which is created from the souls of children born on Saturday, but who passed away before being baptized. It's believed that the *ustrel*, in the invisible form of a spirit, can claw its way out of the grave to drain the blood from livestock, and hide behind the horns or hind legs of its prey. The *ustrel* myth provides a seemingly logical explanation for a sudden loss of sheep and cattle to indeterminate causes.

Luscious Liver Pâté

Serves 6–8

1 pound goose or chicken livers
1 cup chicken broth
1 small onion, sliced
1 sprig fresh rosemary
8 cooked bacon strips, crumbled
½ cup (1 stick) unsalted butter, softened
2 tablespoons brandy or cognac
1 tablespoon Dijon mustard
Kosher salt and freshly cracked black pepper to taste

Cut livers in half and simmer in chicken broth with onion and rosemary for about 15 minutes, until tender. Let cool. Reserve onion and ¼ cup of the broth. Remove leaves from the sprig of rosemary and chop fine.

In a food processor, combine liver, onion, ¼ cup broth, chopped rosemary, crumbled bacon, butter, brandy or cognac, and mustard. Process until smooth. Season to taste with salt and pepper.

Spoon pâté into a covered container. Refrigerate overnight so flavors will blend. Will keep 3 or 4 days in the refrigerator.

Livers, Gizzards, and Hearts—Oh My!

Serves 2

Livers, gizzards, and hearts from 8 chickens
½ cup seasoned flour
2 tablespoons oil
2 tablespoons butter
2 pieces buttered sourdough toast, cut in fourths

Clean liver, gizzards, and hearts well and rinse in water several times until water runs clean. Pat dry and dredge in flour.

Heat oil and butter in a small skillet. Sauté over medium-high heat for about 3 to 4 minutes. Serve with buttered sourdough toast points.

TASTY TIDBIT

PROINSIAS CASSIDY IS THE HIPPEST RENEGADE VAMPIRE EVER TO GRACE THE PAGES OF COMIC BOOKS. HE'S IRISH, HILARIOUS, AND CAN MURDER A GUINNESS LIKE NOBODY'S BUSINESS. CHECK HIM OUT IN THE *PREACHER* COMIC SERIES.

Give Me Some Skin
Serves 6

4 russet potatoes
1/4 cup butter, melted
1/2 cup flour
2 to 3 cups peanut oil
1/2 cup American cheese spread in a jar, melted
1/2 cup bacon crumbles
1/4 cup sliced green onions
1/2 cup sour cream

———————————•—••◆••—•———————————

Preheat oven to 350°F.

Cut the potatoes into wedges with 1" to 2" of skin on them. Toss them with the melted butter, then the flour and arrange them on a baking sheet in one layer. Bake for 20 minutes and remove from the oven.

Scoop the extra potato flesh out of the skins and save it for another use.

Heat the peanut oil in a deep fryer, heavy pot, or wok to 375°F. Fry the potato skins in the oil in batches for 1 to 2 minutes. Drain on paper towels and arrange on plates skin-side down.

Fill the potato boats with melted cheese and bacon crumbles. Sprinkle with green onions, and top with sour cream.

Mincemeat Pie

Serves 10

2 eggs
1 (9-ounce) package mincemeat
1¼ cups water
1 cup granulated sugar
2 heaping tablespoons all-purpose flour
⅛ teaspoon salt
½ teaspoon vanilla extract
1 9" pie pastry shell, baked

Beat the eggs and set aside. Crumble the mincemeat into a bowl. Add the water and let soak for 30 minutes.

Transfer the mincemeat to a medium-sized saucepan and add the sugar, flour, eggs, salt, and vanilla. Place over low heat and bring to a simmer. Stirring constantly, simmer for about 10 minutes or until thick.

Spread the mixture in the pastry shell. Let cool before serving.

TASTY TIDBIT

SPEAKING OF PIES, A SHOUT OUT TO SWEENEY TODD SEEMS APPROPRIATE HERE. THIS DEMON BARBER OF FLEET STREET TOOK REVENGE ON HIS ENEMIES BY SLITTING THEIR THROATS. ONCE DEAD, HIS ACCOMPLICE, MRS. LOVETT, WOULD BAKE THEIR FLESH INTO MEAT PIES AND SELL THEM TO UNSUSPECTING CUSTOMERS. THEY WERE SO DELICIOUS, PEOPLE WERE LITERALLY DYING TO GET THEIR HANDS ON ONE.

Love at First Bite

Mock Chopped Liver

Serves 8

2 shallots
1 pound button mushrooms
2 tablespoons unsalted margarine
½ teaspoon salt
½ teaspoon ground black pepper

Peel and finely chop the shallots. Clean the mushrooms and chop finely.

Melt the margarine in a large skillet over medium heat. Add the shallots and sauté until softened, about 2 minutes.

Add the mushrooms and sauté until the moisture is evaporated, about 10 minutes.

Purée the mushroom mixture in a blender or food processor. Season with the salt and pepper.

Ham with Red-Eye Gravy

Serves 2

2 tablespoons butter
4 slices country ham, about ¼" thick
¾ cup coffee
¼ cup water

Melt butter in a skillet over medium-low to medium heat. Fry ham slices until browned on both sides. Remove ham to a platter; cut in serving-sized pieces and keep warm.

To the same skillet, add the coffee and water. Bring to a boil and continue to boil for 2 to 3 minutes, until reduced slightly, stirring constantly.

Serve gravy with ham and hot cooked grits, along with eggs and other breakfast favorites.

Liver Slivers with Risotto

Serves 6

2 cups beef broth
3 cups water
3 tablespoons olive oil
1 small onion, chopped
1¼ cups Arborio rice
1 teaspoon salt
Freshly ground black pepper to taste
½ pound chicken livers, cleaned and quartered
1 teaspoon soy sauce

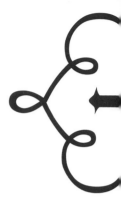

Combine the beef broth and water and heat to a simmer. Place on a back burner over low heat.

Heat 1 tablespoon oil in a large, heavy-bottomed pot over medium heat. Sauté the onion. Add the rice and stir to coat. Sprinkle with salt and pepper.

Add the broth/water combination, ½ cup at a time stirring constantly. Wait for it to hiss before adding more broth.

In a separate pan, heat 2 tablespoons oil. Sauté the chicken livers for about 10 minutes over medium heat. Add the soy sauce.

Gently mix the livers into the rice and serve.

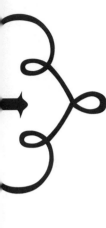

Kidney Bean Casserole

Serves 6

1 teaspoon olive oil
¼ bunch celery
1 yellow onion
½ head romaine lettuce
1 cup puréed carrots
1 cup vegetable stock
1 cup cooked kidney beans
½ cup cooked barley
3 sprigs thyme, leaves only
½ teaspoon dried oregano leaves
½ teaspoon chili powder
Fresh-cracked black pepper, to taste

Preheat oven to 325°F. Grease a casserole or loaf pan with the oil.

Slice the celery and onion. Shred the romaine lettuce.

Blend together the carrot purée and stock.

In the prepared dish, layer the beans, celery, onions, barley, herbs, spices, and the carrot-stock mixture; cover and bake for 30 to 45 minutes. Serve topped with shredded romaine.

Love at First Bite

Blood Sausage
with Cabbage and Apple

Serves 4

¼ pound bacon
1 pound blood sausage
2 tablespoons butter
1 small onion, diced
3 cups cabbage, shredded
2 tart green apples, peeled and sliced
2 tablespoons fresh ground black pepper

———————————◆———◆————————————

Cut the bacon into strips. Skin the blood sausage and cut diagonally into ½" strips.

Heat butter in pan. Add bacon and cook for 2 to 3 minutes and remove. Add blood sausage to the pan, cook for 5 minutes. Remove from direct heat and set aside.

Cook the diced onion for 1 minute; add cabbage, bacon, apple, and juices from the pan. Cover and keep at a low simmer for about 10 minutes.

Arrange the cabbage mixture on a serving plate. Top with the blood sausage and add pepper to taste.

Melt-in-Your-Mouth Tongue Tacos

Makes about 20 tacos

1 beef tongue
1 onion, diced
5 cloves of garlic, crushed
Salt to taste
3 tablespoons olive oil
5 Roma tomatoes
5 peppers (any variety)
2 (10-ounce) packages corn tortillas
1 jar of your favorite salsa

Place the beef tongue in a slow cooker and cover with water. Add half the onion slices and all the garlic. Season with salt. Cover and cook on low for 8 hours or longer. Remove the tongue and shred the meat into strands.

Heat the oil in a skillet over medium heat. Cook the tomatoes and peppers in the hot oil until softened on all sides.

Place cooked tomatoes and peppers in a blender, keeping the oil on the heat; season with salt. Blend the vegetables until still slightly chunky.

Cook the remainder of the onions in the skillet until translucent; stir in the tomato mixture. Cook another 5 to 6 minutes.

Build the tacos by placing shredded tongue meat into a tortilla and spooning salsa over the meat.

Love at First Bite

CHAPTER 9

BLOODLESS BUFFET

Veggie-Friendly Vittles

Buffy's Cheesy Broccoli
Serves 2

8 ounces fresh broccoli
Water, as needed
2 tablespoons butter or margarine
1 tablespoon all-purpose flour
6 tablespoons milk
⅛ teaspoon (or to taste) garlic powder
Salt and pepper, to taste
⅓ cup grated Cheddar cheese
2 tablespoons sour cream

Wash the broccoli and drain. Chop the broccoli into bite-sized pieces, separating the stalks from the florets.

Fill a medium-sized saucepan with 1" of water. Place a metal steamer inside the pan. Make sure the water is not touching the bottom of the steamer. Heat the water to boiling. When the water is boiling, add the broccoli to the steamer. Cover and steam until the broccoli is tender, about 10 minutes. Drain and set aside.

In a medium-sized saucepan, melt the butter over low heat. Stir in the flour. Cook for 2 minutes, stirring continually. Whisk in the milk, garlic powder, and salt and pepper. Bring to a boil over medium heat, whisking continually.

Reduce heat slightly and whisk in the cheese, and then the sour cream. Return to a boil and heat through. Arrange the broccoli on a plate and pour the cheese sauce over the top.

Love at First Bite

Devil Hair Pasta Pesto
Serves 4

⅓ cup pine nuts or walnuts
2 cloves garlic
2 cups packed fresh basil leaves
½ cup olive oil
¼ cup grated Parmesan cheese
½ teaspoon salt
1 pound angel hair pasta
1 teaspoon plain yogurt

Preheat oven to 350°F. Lay the pine nuts or walnuts out in an even layer on an ungreased baking sheet; bake for 10 minutes. Set aside.

In a food processor, chop the garlic and nuts together to make a paste.

Add the basil and 2 tablespoons of the oil to the food processor and process with the nuts and garlic.

With the processor running and the pour hole on the top open, pour the rest of the oil in a thin stream into the basil mixture to form a purée.

Add the Parmesan cheese and salt, and process to blend.

Heat in a saucepan and serve over angel hair pasta.

Store with a teaspoon of plain yogurt stirred into the pesto to prevent it from turning black.

Prince of Darkness Primavera

Serves 4

½ cup diced onion
½ cup diced carrot
¼ cup diced red bell pepper
2 tablespoons olive oil
½ cup vegetable broth
1 cup fresh asparagus spears, cut into 1" pieces
1 cup broccoli florets
½ cup heavy cream
½ cup frozen peas
½ cup grated Parmesan cheese
Salt and pepper to taste

In a 6-quart soup pot, sauté onions, carrots, and red bell pepper in oil until tender.

Add vegetable broth, asparagus, and broccoli. Simmer uncovered for 5 minutes.

Add cream and peas; simmer for 5 minutes more.

Stir in Parmesan cheese and remove from heat.

Season with salt and pepper. Serve sauce over cooked pasta.

Love at First Bite

Serves 4

2 cloves garlic, minced
¼ cup olive oil
1 (28-ounce) can crushed tomatoes
1 teaspoon dried crushed red pepper
½ teaspoon dried oregano
2 tablespoons drained capers
1 cup oil-cured black olives, chopped coarse
5 anchovies, chopped
Salt and pepper to taste
4 servings of cooked pasta
2 tablespoons chopped fresh parsley

In a 6-quart soup pot, sauté garlic in oil for a few minutes.

Add tomatoes, red pepper, and oregano, and cook over medium heat for 10 minutes.

Add capers, black olives, and anchovies and cook for another 5 minutes.

Season sauce with salt (if necessary) and pepper.

Toss cooked pasta in the sauce, and top with chopped fresh parsley.

Alfredo Armand

Serves 4

2 cloves garlic, minced
4 tablespoons butter
2 tablespoons olive oil
1 tablespoon all-purpose flour
1 cup milk
½ cup heavy cream
1 cup grated Parmesan cheese
Salt and pepper to taste

In a 12" pan, sauté garlic in butter and olive oil for 1 minute, then sprinkle with flour.

Stir and cook for 1 minute; then add milk and cook, stirring constantly, until sauce thickens and is bubbling.

Add cream and cook for a minute or two.

Add Parmesan cheese and stir to make a smooth creamy sauce.

Season sauce with salt and pepper. Serve over pasta.

Love at First Bite

Renesmee's Risotto

1 cup diced onion
8 tablespoons butter
2 cups Arborio rice
2 cups water
3 cups vegetable broth
6 tablespoons grated Parmesan cheese
¼ teaspoon pepper
Salt to taste

In a large pot, sauté the onion in the butter until translucent, about 5 minutes.

Add rice to onion and sauté for a few minutes.

In a separate bowl, combine water and vegetable broth. Add ½ cup broth to rice mixture, stirring constantly over medium-high heat until most of the liquid is absorbed. Repeat with the rest of the broth mixture in ½-cup increments. It will take about 20 minutes.

Remove from heat and stir in the Parmesan cheese, pepper, and salt.

TASTY TIDBIT

PLANNING A ROMANTIC DINNER WITH YOUR VAMPIRE CRUSH? REMEMBER TO OMIT THE GARLIC, SALT, INCENSE, AND BELLS WHICH WOULD RUIN THE MOOD. COOK SOMETHING BLAND AND BORING AND SERVE IT BY CANDLELIGHT. AND BE SURE TO HAVE PLENTY OF THE RED STUFF ON HAND TO DRINK— AFTER ALL, YOUR VAMPIRE FRIEND WON'T BE EATING MUCH.

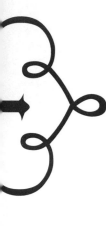

Dungeon Ratatouille

Serves 6

½ cup diced onion
¼ cup diced red bell pepper
¼ cup diced green bell pepper
5 cloves garlic, minced
¼ cup olive oil
2 cups diced eggplant
1 cup diced zucchini
½ cup diced tomatoes, fresh or canned
¼ teaspoon dried tarragon
½ teaspoon dried thyme
1 teaspoon dried basil
Salt and pepper to taste
¼ cup diced oil-cured tomatoes
6 cloves roasted garlic (optional)

Sauté the onion, peppers, and minced garlic in olive oil for 5 minutes.

Add the eggplant and zucchini, toss to coat with oil, and then add the fresh (or canned) tomatoes and herbs.

Cover and simmer for 30 minutes, stirring occasionally.

Season with salt and pepper.

Scatter the oil-cured tomatoes and whole, peeled cloves of roasted garlic on top before serving.

Love at First Bite

Elvira's Eggplant Parmesan
Serves 4

8 (½"-thick) slices eggplant (2 medium-sized eggplants)
1 tablespoon salt
1 cup dry breadcrumbs
1 cup grated Parmesan cheese
1 tablespoon dried oregano
¼ teaspoon pepper

2 eggs
1 cup all-purpose flour
2 cups (1 16-ounce can) tomato sauce
½ cup olive oil
8 slices mozzarella cheese

Preheat oven to 350°F. Sprinkle eggplant with salt and put in a colander to drain for 15 minutes.

In a large bowl, combine bread crumbs, Parmesan cheese, oregano, and pepper.

In a separate bowl, beat eggs with a whisk. Put flour into another bowl.

Spread half of the sauce on the bottom of a 9" × 13" baking dish.

Wipe eggplant slices dry with a paper towel. Dip each eggplant slice first in flour, then egg, then in the bread crumb mixture.

In a large sauté pan, heat the olive oil over medium-high heat. Fry the coated eggplant slices in heated olive oil, turning when bottom side of eggplant is golden brown. Place browned eggplant slices on top of the tomato sauce in the baking dish.

Cover eggplant with remaining tomato sauce. Top each eggplant slice with a slice of mozzarella cheese and bake uncovered for 40 minutes.

Spike's Sweet Potato Fries

Serves 4

4 sweet potatoes
4 cups vegetable oil

Preheat oven to 350°F.

Peel sweet potatoes and slice them into ½"-thick planks lengthwise. Stack the planks and slice them lengthwise into ½"-wide sticks.

Heat oil in a deep pot to 330°F.

Add 1 cup of the sweet potatoes to the hot oil; blanch for 3 minutes. Remove the potatoes from the oil, lay them out on a baking sheet pan, and repeat the process with the rest of the sweet potatoes.

Bake sweet potatoes for 30 to 45 minutes, until they become crisp.

TASTY TIDBIT

SPIKE FIRST SHOWED AS BUFFY'S ARCH NEMESIS IN SEASON TWO. ALONG WITH HIS VAMPY GIRLFRIEND DRUSILLA (SID AND NANCY WANNABES), THESE TWO CAUSE MAJOR PROBLEMS FOR THE SLAYER AND HER FRIENDS. FANS LOVE SPIKE FOR HIS MEMORABLE QUOTES AND ONE-LINERS.

Love at First Bite

Brussels Sprouts to Die For

Serves 2

16 fresh Brussels sprouts
Olive oil, as needed
Coarse sea salt, as needed
Water, as needed

Preheat the oven to 375°F. Rinse Brussels sprouts under cold, running water. Remove stems and outer leaves. Place sprouts in an ovenproof baking pan.

Generously sprinkle with olive oil.

Generously sprinkle with coarse sea salt or kosher salt

Bake uncovered 45 minutes to 1 hour until tender.

Marius's Mac and Cheese

Serves 6

4 tablespoons butter
¼ cup all-purpose flour
1 teaspoon dry mustard
2¾ cups milk
1 teaspoon salt
⅛ teaspoon pepper
3 cups shredded Cheddar cheese
16 ounces elbow macaroni, cooked and drained
1 cup dry bread crumbs

Preheat oven to 350°F. Butter a 9" × 13" baking dish.

Melt the butter in a medium-sized saucepan. Stir in the flour and dry mustard; cook (stirring) over medium heat for 2 minutes.

Add the milk and whisk constantly over medium heat until mixture thickens. Stir in the salt and pepper. Remove from heat. Stir in the cheese and let the mixture sit for a minute.

Pour cooked macaroni into the casserole dish; add cheese sauce. Mix until macaroni is coated with cheese. Sprinkle bread crumbs on top of the casserole and bake for 45 minutes, until browned and bubbly on the edges.

TASTY TIDBIT

MARIUS IS THE MAIN CHARACTER IN ANNE RICE'S NOVEL *BLOOD AND GOLD*. THE CREATOR OF ARMAND AND PANDORA, HE IS ONE OF THE OLDEST VAMPIRES KNOWN TO STILL SURVIVE.

Love at First Bite

Rapturous Rice Pilaf

Serves 4

8 tablespoons unsalted butter
½ cup diced onion
1 cup long-grain rice
12 ounces vegetable broth
½ teaspoon salt
¼ teaspoon white pepper
1 bay leaf

Preheat oven to 350°F.

In a saucepan over medium heat, melt butter. Sauté the onion in butter until tender.

Add rice; sauté for 3 to 5 minutes with the onion.

Pour rice mixture into a 9" × 13" baking dish. Add vegetable broth, salt, pepper, and bay leaf. Stir to incorporate.

Cover and bake for 45 minutes. Remove bay leaf before serving.

Sanguine Spaghetti Squash

Serves 6

2 spaghetti squashes
1 cup water
¼ cup olive oil
Fresh-cracked black pepper

Preheat oven to 350°F.

Cut the squashes in half; remove and discard the seeds. Place the squashes cut-side down in a baking dish and pour in the water. Cover the baking dish with a lid or aluminum foil. Steam in the oven for 45 minutes to 1 hour, until fork tender.

Remove from oven and let cool slightly. Scrape out the insides of the squashes, spooning the flesh into a serving bowl. Drizzle with olive oil and sprinkle with pepper.

TASTY TIDBIT

VAMPIRES, WITHOUT QUESTION, ARE ENTIRELY INTIMIDATING. AND THEY HAVE EVERY RIGHT TO BE, GIVEN THE VARYING RANGE OF "SUPER POWERS" THEY CAN POSSESS SUCH AS SUPERHUMAN STRENGTH, PHYSICAL AGILITY, ACUTE VISION, A MAGNIFIED SENSE OF SMELL AND HEARING, HYPNOSIS, AND THE ABILITY TO SEE THE FUTURE.

Love at First Bite

Suffering Suck-o-Tash

Serves 6

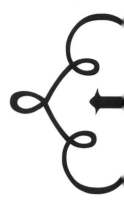

½ pound fresh lima beans
2 ears fresh corn
1 large yellow onion
1 red pepper
1 teaspoon olive oil
Freshly cracked black pepper, to taste
1 tablespoon flour
½ cup skim milk
½ cup vegetable broth

Cook the beans and corn separately in boiling water until just tender (not quite done). Remove the corn kernels from the cobs. Dice the onion and red pepper into small pieces.

In a large saucepan, heat the oil to medium temperature, add the onion, and sauté until light golden in color. Add the red pepper and cook for 1 minute. Season with black pepper.

Add the beans and corn, sprinkle with flour, and stir. Whisk in the milk and broth; simmer at low heat for approximately 30 to 45 minutes, until the beans and corn are thoroughly cooked.

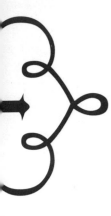

Bella's Favorite Mushroom Ravioli

Serves 6

2 shallots
2 cloves garlic
2 portobello mushrooms
1 tablespoon olive oil
¼ cup dry white wine
1 teaspoon unsalted cold butter
Freshly cracked black pepper, to taste
1½ cups pasta dough
1 cup pesto

Finely dice the shallots and mince the garlic. Clean off the mushrooms with damp paper towels, scrape out the black membrane on the underside of the cap, and dice them into large pieces.

Heat the oil to medium temperature in a large sauté pan. Add the shallots, garlic, and mushrooms; sauté for approximately 5 minutes. Add the wine and let it reduce by half. Add the butter and remove from heat. Season with pepper and allow to cool thoroughly.

Roll the pasta dough at least ¹/₁₆" thick and cut into 3" to 4" squares or circles. Put a teaspoon of filling in the middle of the ravioli. Fold each square in half and seal tightly with a fork. Cook the ravioli in boiling water until al dente (approximately 5 to 7 minutes), then drain and serve with the pesto.

Love at First Bite

Hellfire Noodles

Serves 4–6

15–20 (or to taste) Thai bird chilies, stemmed and seeded
5–10 (or to taste) cloves garlic
1 pound pre-sliced fresh rice noodles
2 tablespoons vegetable oil
2 tablespoons fish sauce
2 tablespoons sweet black soy sauce
1 tablespoon oyster sauce
1 teaspoon white pepper
1½ tablespoons sugar
1 (8-ounce) can bamboo shoots, drained
1½ cups loosed-packed basil and/or mint

Place the chilies and garlic cloves in a food processor and process until thoroughly mashed together; set aside.

Bring a kettle of water to a boil. Place the noodles in a large colander and pour the hot water over them. Carefully unfold and separate the noodles; set aside.

Heat the oil in a wok or large skillet over medium-high heat. When it is quite hot, carefully add the reserved chili-garlic mixture and stir-fry for 15 seconds to release the aromas.

Stir in the fish sauce, soy sauce, oyster sauce, white pepper, and sugar.

Add the noodles and continue to stir-fry for 30 seconds, tossing them with the other ingredients.

Add the bamboo shoots and cook for another minute.

Turn off the heat and add the basil.

Van Helsing's Veggie Rolls

Serves 6

2 cups coleslaw mix
1 teaspoon sesame oil
½ cup plus 1 tablespoon soy sauce
Pinch sugar
½ teaspoon salt

¼ teaspoon pepper
18 spring roll wrappers
1 egg, beaten
3 cups vegetable oil
¼ cup rice wine vinegar

Mix the coleslaw mix with the sesame oil, 1 tablespoon soy sauce, sugar, salt, and pepper.

Lay a spring roll wrapper flat with the points facing like a diamond shape. Put 1 to 2 tablespoons of the filling on the bottom third of the wrapper. Fold up the bottom corner over the filling, fold in the two side corners over the filling. Brush the top corner with the beaten egg and roll the rest of the way tightly, encasing the filling in the wrapper. Repeat.

Heat the oil in a deep fryer to 365°F. Add the rolls and fry until golden. Remove from the oil and drain on paper towels.

Combine ½ cup soy sauce and ¼ cup rice wine vinegar and serve with the hot spring rolls for dipping.

TASTY TIDBIT

THE DUTCH PROFESSOR, DOCTOR, AND PHILOSOPHER TURNED VAMPIRE HUNTER IS UNQUESTIONABLY THE HERO OF DRACULA. IT IS VAN HELSING WHO DISCOVERS DRACULA'S STRENGTHS, WEAKNESSES, AND HOW TO DESTROY HIM.

Love at First Bite

Nosfera-Tofu Treat

Serves 6

1 teaspoon sesame oil
1 pound extra-firm tofu, drained and cut into ½" cubes
1 tablespoon rice vinegar
2 tablespoons low-sodium soy sauce
¼ teaspoon ground ginger

Coat a skillet with nonstick spray. Add sesame oil and tofu to skillet and sauté on medium-high heat for 6 to 7 minutes or until brown.

Remove tofu, mix with remaining ingredients, and chill.

TASTY TIDBIT

THE TERM *NOSFERATU* IS DERIVED FROM THE GREEK WORD *NOSOPHOROS*, WHICH TRANSLATES TO "PLAGUE CARRIER." THE CONFUSION THAT A NOSFERATU IS A VAMPIRE IS OFTEN ATTRIBUTED TO AN 1888 TRAVELOGUE CONTAINING TRANSYLVANIAN FOLKLORE WRITTEN BY EMILY GERARD. CALLED *THE LAND BEYOND THE FOREST*, IT WAS KNOWN TO HAVE BEEN USED BY BRAM STOKER IN HIS RESEARCH FOR *DRACULA*. AS SUCH, STOKER USED THE TERM TO ALSO MEAN VAMPIRE, WHEN IN FACT, "PLAGUE CARRIER" IS MORE ACCURATE AS ACCORDING TO LORE, VAMPIRES WERE SOMETIMES BLAMED AS THE CAUSE OF PLAGUES.

Vlad's Veggie Quesadillas

Serves 6

6 (8") whole-wheat or multigrain tortillas
2½ cups shredded Cheddar cheese
2 cups mixed shredded or cut-up vegetables
½ cup salsa

Preheat a large skillet or griddle over medium heat and spray it lightly with nonstick cooking spray.

Place 1 tortilla on a flat surface and sprinkle it with ½ cup cheese. Put about ⅓ cup vegetables and 2 tablespoons salsa on half of the tortilla and fold it over to close. Place the tortilla onto the griddle and heat until the first side turns golden and the cheese melts. Flip over to cook the second side. Repeat with the remaining ingredients, spraying with nonstick cooking spray as needed and not letting the griddle overheat.

Cut the quesadillas into serving portions and serve hot.

Love at First Bite

Fiery Indian Potatoes

Serves 6

6 large potatoes, peeled and cubed
3 tablespoons vegetable oil, or more as needed
5 dried red chilies, or to taste, crushed
1 tablespoon mustard seeds
1 teaspoon ground turmeric
1 teaspoon red chili powder
Salt and freshly ground black pepper to taste
1 tablespoon ground coriander
1 cup chopped fresh cilantro for garnish

Steam the potato cubes until just tender.

Heat the oil in a large skillet or wok, and sauté the potatoes for 2 minutes. Add the chilies, mustard seeds, turmeric, chili powder, salt, and pepper and continue cooking over medium heat, stirring, until the seasonings are well mixed and the potatoes begin to brown.

Stir in the coriander, garnish with the cilantro, and serve.

Alice's Stuffed Artichokes

Serves 2

1 cup water
½ cup pomegranate juice
1 teaspoon butter
1 cup uncooked couscous
¾ cup toasted pine nuts
10 dried apricots, coarsely chopped
½ cup cilantro leaves
Pinch salt
2 very large globe artichokes, trimmed and cooked

Combine 1 cup water and the pomegranate juice in a saucepan and heat to boiling, then stir in the butter and couscous. Remove from the heat and cover; set aside for 5 minutes.

Meanwhile, in a mixing bowl, combine the pine nuts, apricots, cilantro leaves, and salt, stirring well. Fold in the couscous.

Part the artichoke leaves to expose the center. Using a spoon, scoop out the central thistles, or choke, and discard. Spoon the couscous mixture into the artichokes, mounding it up to fill them completely. Serve hot or at room temperature.

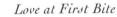

Gothic Gnocchi

Serves 4

1 (17.6-ounce) package fresh gnocchi
1 bunch broccolini, chopped and cooked
10 baby purple potatoes, cooked and cubed
1 (13¾-ounce) can artichoke hearts, drained and quartered
3 tablespoons capers
½ cup olive oil
3 tablespoons red wine vinegar
2 tablespoons pesto
Salt and freshly ground black pepper to taste

Cook the gnocchi according to package directions, drain, and put into a serving bowl. Add the broccolini, potatoes, artichoke hearts, and capers.

Whisk together the oil, vinegar, pesto, salt, and pepper. Pour over the vegetables and toss to combine. Serve.

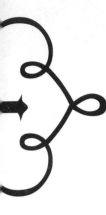

You Never Slaw It Coming
Serves 4

1 (1-pound) package fresh udon noodles
6 ounces broccoli slaw
3 tablespoons pickled ginger
⅓ cup soy sauce
2 tablespoon brown rice vinegar
1 tablespoon toasted sesame oil
1 tablespoon mayonnaise
1 tablespoon sugar
Sprinkles of rice seasoning for garnish

Bring a large pot of water to a boil and cook the noodles for about 1 minute. Drain and rinse in cold water. Set aside to cool slightly.

Add the broccoli slaw and the ginger to a salad bowl. Mix together the soy sauce, vinegar, sesame oil, mayonnaise, and sugar, stirring to combine well. Add the noodles to the bowl and toss the mixture together until well combined. Add the dressing and toss again.

Sprinkle with rice seasoning and serve.

Embrace the Darkness Frittata

Serves 4

2 tablespoons olive oil
1 onion, finely chopped
1½ cups frozen broccoli florets, thawed
6 eggs, beaten
⅓ cup whole milk
½ teaspoon garlic salt
⅛ teaspoon white pepper
Dash red pepper flakes
1 cup shredded Gouda cheese

Preheat broiler. In large ovenproof skillet, heat olive oil over medium heat. Add onion, cook and stir for 3 to 4 minutes, until crisp-tender.

Meanwhile, drain broccoli thoroughly and press between paper towels to remove more liquid. Add broccoli to skillet; cook and stir for 2 to 3 minutes, until hot. In a large bowl, beat eggs with milk, garlic salt, white pepper, and red pepper flakes to taste. Pour into skillet.

Cook over medium heat, covered, for 4 to 5 minutes. Remove cover and run spatula under eggs to loosen, cook until edges are puffed and center is almost set. Sprinkle with cheese. Place skillet under broiler and broil for 2 to 4 minutes, until eggs are set and cheese is melted.

Vampirella's Veggie Pancakes

Serves 4

8 crepes
2 tablespoons olive oil
1 cup refrigerated hash brown potatoes
1 cup frozen baby peas
½ teaspoon dried tarragon leaves
½ teaspoon salt
⅛ teaspoon pepper
1 cup sour cream, divided
1½ cups shredded Gruyère cheese

Prepare crepes or defrost if frozen. In medium saucepan, heat olive oil over medium heat. Add potatoes and peas; cook and stir until vegetables are hot and potatoes begin to brown. Remove from heat and sprinkle with tarragon, salt, and pepper.

Add half of the sour cream and mix well. Fill crepes with this mixture; roll to enclose filling. Place in microwave-safe baking dish. Spread crepes with remaining sour cream and sprinkle with cheese.

Microwave, covered, for 3 to 6 minutes on 70 percent power, rotating once during cooking time, until cheese is melted and crepes are hot. Serve immediately.

Love at First Bite

CHAPTER 10

NOCTURNAL NIBBLES

Sweets for the
Midnight Hour

Angel of Death Biscuits
Makes 24 biscuits

1 package active dry yeast (¼ ounce)
¼ cup warm water (about 110°F)
5 to 5¼ cups all-purpose flour
¼ cup granulated sugar
2 teaspoons baking powder
1 teaspoon baking soda
1 tablespoon salt
¾ cup shortening, chilled
2 cups buttermilk, at room temperature
4 tablespoons butter, chilled
Melted butter for brushing tops

Dissolve the yeast in ¼ cup of warm water. Set aside.

In a large mixing bowl, combine flour, sugar, baking powder, baking soda, and salt; stir to blend. Cut in shortening until mixture resembles coarse meal, with some small pea-sized pieces remaining. Stir in yeast mixture and buttermilk, blending well.

Turn dough out onto a lightly floured surface; knead a few times with floured hands, adding a little more flour if the dough is too sticky to handle. Pat into a circle about ½" thick. Cut out rounds with 2½" biscuit cutter. Place biscuits on a lightly greased baking sheet. Put the remaining scraps of dough together, pat out, cut, and repeat until all of the dough is used. Cover uncooked biscuits with a dish cloth and let rise in a draft-free place for about 30 to 45 minutes.

Bake at 400°F for about 15 to 20 minutes, until tops are browned. Remove from oven and brush with melted butter while biscuits are still hot.

Love at First Bite

Cat Tongues

Makes 36 cookies

½ cup softened unsalted butter
⅔ cup sugar
3 egg whites, room temperature
1½ teaspoons vanilla extract
1½ cups all-purpose flour
6 ounces bittersweet chocolate, melted

Preheat oven to 400°F. Lightly grease baking sheets.

Cream butter and sugar until light and fluffy. Beat egg whites and vanilla until stiff peaks form; fold into butter mixture. Carefully sift flour over top; fold in.

Put dough in a pastry bag and pipe 3" long cookies.

Bake 10 minutes. Cool.

Dip one end of cookie in melted chocolate; allow chocolate to set.

Coffin Cake

Serves 12

½ cup dark brown sugar

2 teaspoons cinnamon

3⅓ cups all-purpose flour

1 cup cold butter

1½ cups sugar

3 eggs

2 teaspoons baking powder

1 teaspoon baking soda

½ teaspoon salt

1 cup sour cream

Preheat oven to 350°F. Butter a Bundt pan.

Make filling by combining the brown sugar, cinnamon, ⅓ cup of the flour, and ¼ cup of the butter with fingertips until crumbly. Set aside.

Cream together ¾ cup butter and sugar until fluffy. Add eggs one at a time and beat them in to form a smooth batter. Separately, mix together 3 cups flour, baking powder, baking soda, and salt, using a whisk.

Add flour mixture alternately with sour cream to the butter/egg mixture until all is incorporated. Layer half the batter in the pan; sprinkle it with the filling mixture. Layer the rest of the batter on top.

Bake 50 minutes, or until a toothpick inserted comes out clean.

TASTY TIDBIT

THE CONCEPT OF HAVING A COFFIN IS GENERALLY BELIEVED TO HAVE BEEN A LOGICAL NECESSITY IN KEEPING ANIMALS— OR IN THE CASE OF FOLKLORE, VAMPIRES—AWAY FROM THE DEAD.

Love at First Bite

Legosi's Lemony Oatmeal Cookies

Makes 50 cookies

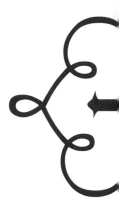

½ cup butter or margarine
1 cup granulated sugar
1 egg
1 teaspoon vanilla extract
1 teaspoon lemon extract
½ teaspoon baking soda
½ teaspoon baking powder
½ teaspoon salt
1 cup all-purpose flour
½ cup sweetened shredded coconut
1 cup quick-cooking oats

Preheat oven to 350°F. Grease a baking sheet well.

Cream together the butter and sugar. Beat the egg with the vanilla and lemon extract. Beat into the butter and sugar mixture until creamy.

Sift the baking soda, baking powder, and salt into the flour. Add to the butter mixture and beat until well blended. Stir in the coconut and oats.

Use a teaspoon to drop the dough onto the baking tray, placing them well apart (about 15 cookies per tray). For best results, don't drop more than a level teaspoon, as the cookies expand quite a bit.

Bake for about 6 minutes, until lightly browned around the edges. Let cool. Store in an airtight container.

Gran Stackhouse's Pecan Pie

Serves 8

1 pre-made pie crust
3 large eggs
1 cup light corn syrup
⅛ teaspoon salt
1 teaspoon vanilla extract
1 cup light brown sugar, firmly packed
2 tablespoons melted butter
1¼ cups pecan halves

Fit crust into a 9" pie pan. Heat oven to 400°F.

In a mixing bowl, beat the eggs. Whisk in the corn syrup, salt, vanilla, brown sugar, and melted butter, blending well. Stir in pecan halves or pieces.

Pour the pecan mixture into the unbaked pie shell.

Bake pie at 400°F for 10 minutes. Reduce heat to 350°F and continue baking for 25 to 30 minutes longer. If the crust becomes too dark, cover the edge with a protective pie shield or fashion a ring of foil to lightly cover the pastry edge. When the pie is finished, the edge of the filling should be slightly puffed and firm, and the center should move only slightly.

Serve with whipped cream or vanilla ice cream.

Love at First Bite

Red Devil Demon Cake

Serves 8

2 cups packed brown sugar
1 cup milk
3 (1-ounce) squares unsweetened chocolate
½ cup vegetable shortening
1 teaspoon vanilla extract
½ teaspoon red food coloring
3 eggs
2 cups sifted flour
2 teaspoon baking soda
½ teaspoon salt

Preheat oven to 350°F. Line the bottom of two 8" round cake pans with wax paper and grease the sides.

In a saucepan, combine 1 cup of the brown sugar, ½ cup of the milk, and the chocolate over very low heat until the chocolate melts. Remove from the heat and let cool.

In a large bowl, stir the shortening to soften. Gradually add the remaining 1 cup brown sugar and cream until light and fluffy. Add the vanilla and red food coloring, mixing well. Beat in the eggs one at a time, beating well after each addition. Blend in the chocolate mixture.

In another bowl, sift together the flour, baking soda, and salt. Add the flour mixture to the creamed mixture alternately with the remaining ½ cup milk, beginning and ending with the flour mixture. Beat well after each addition. Pour into the prepared pans.

Bake for about 25 minutes, or until a knife comes out clean. Cool on racks.

Edward's Sparkle Cake

Serves 10

1 package angel food cake mix
1 package (3 ounces) strawberry Jell-O
1 cup boiling water
1 package (1 pound) frozen strawberries
1 cup whipping cream
2 tablespoons sugar
Fresh strawberries (optional)

Bake the angel food cake as directed on the package. Let cool.

In a large bowl, dissolve the Jell-O in the boiling water and add the frozen block of strawberries, stirring to break up and mix the berries.

Place the cake, widest side down, on the serving plate. Cut a 1"-thick layer from the top and set aside. Cut around the cake 1" from the outer edge to within 1" from the bottom. Gently remove the section of cake between the cuts, and tear it into small pieces. Fold the pieces into the strawberry mixture and pour the mixture into the cake shell. Place the reserved cake layer on top.

Whip the cream until thick and stir in the sugar. Spread over the top and sides of the cake. Decorate with fresh strawberries, if desired. Refrigerate for a least 1 hour before serving.

Harker's Hermits

Makes 30 cookies

1 cup packed light brown sugar
¼ cup margarine, softened
¼ cup vegetable shortening
¼ cup cold, strong brewed coffee
1 egg
½ teaspoon ground cinnamon
½ teaspoon ground nutmeg
1¾ cups flour
½ teaspoon baking soda
½ teaspoon salt
1¼ cups raisins
¾ cup nuts, chopped

Preheat oven to 375°F.

In a large bowl, mix together the brown sugar, margarine, shortening, coffee, egg, cinnamon, and nutmeg. Stir in flour, baking soda, salt, raisins, and nuts. Mix well.

Drop the dough by rounded teaspoonfuls 2" apart on an ungreased baking sheet.

Bake for 8 to 10 minutes, or until almost no indentation remains when touched. Immediately remove to racks to cool.

Bram's Blueberry Buckle
Serves 8–10

½ cup vegetable shortening
1 cup sugar
1 egg, well beaten
2½ cups sifted flour
1½ teaspoons baking powder
¼ teaspoon salt
½ cup milk
1 pint blueberries
½ teaspoon ground cinnamon
¼ cup butter or margarine, softened

Preheat an oven to 350°F. Grease an 11½" × 7½" baking pan.

In a bowl, cream together the shortening and ½ cup of the sugar. Add the egg and mix well. Sift together 2 cups of the sifted flour, the baking powder, and the salt and add to the creamed mixture alternately with the milk. Pour into the prepared pan. Sprinkle the blueberries evenly over the batter.

In a bowl, combine the remaining ½ cup sugar and ½ cup flour and the cinnamon. Add the butter and cut in with a pastry blender until crumbly. Sprinkle over the blueberries.

Bake for 45 to 50 minutes, or until blueberry mixture bubbles. Let cool slightly on a rack. Cut into 8 to 10 squares. Serve warm.

Love at First Bite

Come Hither Chocolate Cake
Serves 8

¾ cup sugar
1 cup flour
2 teaspoons baking powder
⅛ teaspoon salt
1 (1-ounce) square semisweet chocolate, melted and cooled,
or 2 tablespoons unsweetened cocoa powder
2 tablespoons butter or margarine
1 teaspoon vanilla extract
½ cup milk
½ cup packed brown sugar
½ cup granulated sugar
4 teaspoons unsweetened cocoa powder
1 cup cold, strong brewed coffee
Ice cream or whipped cream

Preheat oven to 350°F. Grease an 8" or 9" square cake pan.

Sift together the granulated sugar, the flour, baking powder, and salt into a bowl. Add the chocolate, butter, vanilla, and milk and mix well. Pour into the prepared pan. Sprinkle the brown sugar, the remaining ½ cup granulated sugar, and the cocoa over the batter. Finally, pour the cold coffee evenly over the top. Do not mix.

Bake for 30 to 35 minutes, or until a knife comes out clean.

This cake is best served hot. Serve the cake portion on the bottom. Accompany with ice cream or with whipped cream.

Black Satin Cape Cake

Serves 10

½ cup butter or margarine

4 tablespoons unsweetened cocoa powder

½ cup vegetable oil

1 cup water

2 cups flour

2 cups sugar

½ cup buttermilk

2 eggs

1 teaspoon baking soda

1 teaspoon vanilla extract

Preheat oven to 400°F. Grease a 9" × 13" pan.

Put butter, cocoa, oil, and water in a saucepan and bring to a boil. Remove from the heat. Sift together the flour and sugar into a large bowl. Pour the chocolate sauce over the flour mixture and mix well.

In another bowl, beat together the buttermilk, eggs, baking soda, and vanilla and add to the chocolate mixture. Pour into the pan.

Bake for 20 minutes, or until a knife comes out clean.

Remove the cake from the oven and frost it immediately.

Black Satin Frosting

½ cup butter or margarine

1½ cups buttermilk

2 tablespoons unsweetened cocoa powder

1 pound confectioner's sugar

½ teaspoon salt

½ teaspoon vanilla extract

Put the butter, buttermilk, and cocoa in a saucepan and bring to a boil. Remove from the heat and add the sugar, salt, and vanilla, mixing well.

Love at First Bite

Angel's Strawberry Cake
Serves 10

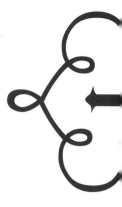

2 pints strawberries, stemmed and sliced
1 (10-ounce) package frozen passion fruit purée, thawed
2 cups sugar
2 tablespoons unflavored gelatin
10 egg whites
2 cups whipping cream, whipped to soft peaks
1 angel food cake

In a large saucepan over low heat, combine the strawberries, passion fruit, and 1 cup of the sugar. Heat until warm. Place the mixture in a food processor and add the gelatin while the mixture is still warm. Purée until smooth. Let cool for 15 minutes.

Meanwhile, place the egg whites in a mixing bowl. Using an electric mixer set on medium speed, beat the egg whites while gradually adding the remaining 1 cup sugar. When the whites hold soft peaks, increase the speed to high and whip until stiff peaks form. Gently fold the egg whites into the purée. Follow with the whipped cream.

Cut the angel food cake in half horizontally. Spread the mousse onto the bottom layer, top with the second layer, and freeze for 30 minutes before serving.

Lady's Fingers

Makes 30 cookies

1¼ cups cake flour

½ cup granulated sugar

6 egg yolks, at room temperature

1 teaspoon vanilla extract

4 egg whites, at room temperature

1 cup confectioner's sugar

Preheat oven to 350°F. Line 2 baking sheets with wax paper.

In a large bowl, sift together the flour and ¼ cup of the granulated sugar; set aside. In another bowl, using an electric mixer set on high speed, beat the egg yolks until the mixture thickens and is pale yellow, 3 to 5 minutes. Add the vanilla and beat briefly. Set aside.

In a large bowl, using clean beaters, beat the egg whites with an electric mixer set on low speed until small bubbles appear, about 30 seconds. Increase the speed to medium and add 1 teaspoon of the granulated sugar. Continue whipping until soft, white peaks form, about 1 minute. Add the rest of the granulated sugar in a steady stream. Continue whipping until thicker, stiffer, glossy peaks form, about 2 minutes.

Using a rubber spatula, gently fold the yolks in to the egg white mixture with a few strokes. Take about one-third of the flour mixture, sprinkle it over the surface of the eggs, and gently fold in with the spatula. Repeat until the ingredients are blended.

Place the batter into a pastry bag fitted with a 2" round tip. Pipe the batter into 5"-long ladyfingers, spacing them ½" apart. You'll have about 15 ladyfingers on each sheet. With a sifter, gently dust the confectioner's sugar over the ladyfingers.

Bake for about 10 minutes, or until the ladyfingers spring back when lightly touched. When done, remove the baking sheets from the oven and remove the wax paper with the ladyfingers on it to a wire rack. After 5 minutes, gently remove the ladyfingers to the rack to cool thoroughly. To store, place in a plastic container with wax paper between the layers.

Love at First Bite

New Moon Cakes

Serves 8

2 cups all-purpose flour
½ cup sugar
Pinch of salt
1 cup butter, softened
2 egg yolks
2 cups sweet red bean paste

In a bowl, combine flour, sugar, and salt. Add softened butter and blend mixture with 2 knives or a pastry blender. Add egg yolks and mix well.

Roll dough into a ball and cover with plastic wrap. Refrigerate 1 hour.

Remove dough from refrigerator. With hands, remove small pieces of dough and roll into 36 balls. Place balls on greased cookie sheets. Flatten each in the center with the back of a teaspoon. Fill each indentation with red bean paste. Bake at 350°F for 20 minutes or until cakes turn light brown.

TASTY TIDBIT

PERHAPS THE MOST FRIGHTENING PART OF WEREWOLVES IS THEIR ABILITY TO CHANGE BACK AND FORTH FROM HUMAN TO WOLF FORM. *SHAPESHIFTING* HAS LONG BEEN A MAINSTAY OF SUPERNATURAL BEHAVIOR, BUT IN THE CASE OF WEREWOLVES THE CAPACITY TO CHANGE ISN'T NECESSARILY DESIRED, AND IT CAN BE A DIFFICULT PROBLEM FOR MERE MORTALS TO UNDO.

Come Closer Kumquat Pie

Serves 6

1 (14-ounce) can condensed milk
¾ cup lime juice
1 pint fresh kumquats, stemmed and chopped
1 prepared 9" graham cracker crust
1 cup heavy cream
2 tablespoons sugar

Combine the condensed milk with the lime juice, mixing together well. Fold in the kumquats and spoon the mixture into the crust. Refrigerate for at least 6 hours or overnight, or until the filling is firm.

Before serving, using chilled beaters, whip the cream until it begins to thicken and slowly stream in the sugar. When the mixture is thick, spread it evenly over the pie and serve.

Love at First Bite

Passion Pudding

Serves 6

1 (14-ounce) can coconut milk, well chilled
1 (14-ounce) can sweetened condensed milk
1 (16.8-ounce) bottle passion fruit concentrate
2 cups cubed pound cake
1 cup toasted shredded coconut
Fresh fruits such as cut-up strawberries or blueberries as garnish

Carefully scoop out the thick top layer of coconut milk and put it into a bowl. Don't use the coconut water at the bottom of the can.

Beat the milk until it thickens and resembles partially whipped heavy cream. Stir in the condensed milk.

Fill the condensed milk can with the passion fruit concentrate and pour it into the mixing bowl. Stir well to combine the milks and juice.

Line the bottom of a 2-quart dessert bowl with the pound cake. Pour the passion fruit mixture over top and chill until firm.

To serve, sprinkle the toasted coconut over the mousse, spoon the mixture into individual bowls, and garnish with fresh fruits as desired.

Undead Gingerbread Men
Makes 12–36 cookies

½ cup granulated sugar
½ cup solid vegetable shortening
1 large egg
½ teaspoon salt
1 teaspoon baking powder
½ teaspoon baking soda
1 teaspoon ground ginger
1½ teaspoons ground cinnamon
1 teaspoon ground cloves
½ cup light molasses
2¼ cups all-purpose flour
Prepared frostings
Candies for trimmings

Preheat oven to 350°F.

In a large mixing bowl, beat together the sugar and shortening. Add the egg, salt, baking powder, baking soda, ginger, cinnamon, cloves, and molasses. Add the flour ½ cup at a time, beating until dough forms.

Shape the dough into a ball, wrap in plastic wrap, and chill until firm, at least 1 hour.

On a floured surface, roll out the dough to ¼" thickness. Using a gingerbread man cookie cutter, cut out the cookies. Place on an ungreased cookie sheet at least 1" apart.

Bake the cookies in batches for 8 to 10 minutes for small cookies, 12 to 15 minutes for larger cookies. Transfer the baking sheet to a wire rack to cool. Frost and decorate.

Love at First Bite

I Vant S'mores

Serves 4

4 large marshmallows
2 chocolate bars
4 sheets of graham crackers

Over an open flame, toast a marshmallow on a stick until it is brown and melted.

Break a graham cracker sheet in half and place a square of chocolate on one half.

Place the melted marshmallow on top of the chocolate and put the other graham half on the marshmallow.

Repeat steps for three more s'mores.

Spider Bites

Makes as many as you like

Flat chocolate wafer cookies
Small tube of white decorator gel
Toothpicks
Gummy spiders

———————————

Place chocolate wafer cookies on a cookie sheet or flat tray.

Using decorator gel, draw 3 circles on the cookie, one large one around the outside rim, a smaller one on the inside, and an even smaller one in the middle.

Using your toothpick, start at the inside middle of the cookie and run the toothpick all the way to the outside edge. Do this about 4 times around the cookie. This will create a "web."

Place gummy spiders on top of your web.

Renfield's Rice Treats

Serves 12

3 tablespoons of butter or margarine
1 (10-ounce) package of marshmallows
6 cups of rice cereal

Melt the butter or margarine in a saucepan. Add the marshmallows to the melted butter and stir until marshmallows are completely melted.

Remove the pan from the heat and stir in the rice cereal. Make sure all of the cereal is coated with the marshmallow and butter mixture.

Pour into a 13" × 9" pan and spread out evenly. When it cools, cut into squares.

TASTY TIDBIT

IN MANY OF THE DRACULA-BASED FILMS, IT'S RENFIELD WHO HAS COMPLETELY LOST HIS MIND AND IDENTITY TO DRACULA, A FACT THAT MAKES HIM ONE OF THE MORE INTRIGUING CHARACTERS. OBSESSED WITH CONSUMING SPIDERS, FLIES, AND SMALL BIRDS, RENFIELD IS USED AS A CONDUIT BY DRACULA TO GAIN ENTRANCE TO THE ASYLUM.

Pandora's Plum Pudding
Makes 3 loaves

2 cups shortening
2 cups brown sugar
4 eggs
1 cup molasses
1 cup brandy
2 lemons
2 cups flour
½ teaspoon nutmeg
½ teaspoon ground ginger
½ teaspoon ground cloves
½ teaspoon cinnamon
½ pound orange peel
½ pound lemon peel
1 cup bread crumbs
1 pound currants
½ pound golden raisins

Cream the shortening and the sugar. Add the eggs, molasses, and brandy. Squeeze the lemons and add the lemon juice.

Sift the flour with the spices. Mince the orange and lemon peel. Mix the minced peel, bread crumbs, currants, and raisins together. Stir this into the dry ingredients.

Stir the dry ingredients into the liquid mixture.

Fill three greased and floured loaf pans ½ to ¾ full with the batter. Loosely cover each dish with foil. Place on a trivet or rack in the slow cooker, and pour water around the base of the trivet.

Cover and heat on a high setting for 2 to 3 hours.

Love at First Bite

Midnight Star Cake

Makes 3 loaves

1 cup flour	3 cups currants
½ teaspoon ground cloves	2 cups raisins
½ teaspoon ground ginger	1 cup dried cherries
½ tablespoon allspice	1 cup butter
½ teaspoon cinnamon	1 cup sugar
1 orange	5 eggs
1 lemon	¼ cup molasses
1 cup citron	½ cup brandy

Sift the flour; blend with the spices. Grate the orange and lemon peels; mince the citron. Add the grated peels, citron, currants, raisins, and cherries to the dry ingredients.

Cut the butter into the sugar; stir in the eggs, molasses, and brandy. Squeeze the juice from the remaining (grated) lemon and add to the liquid mixture.

Combine the liquid and dry mixtures.

Grease and flour three loaf pans or the equivalent. Fill the baking dishes ½ to ¾ full; cover each dish with foil or a glass or ceramic lid. Arrange the dishes on a trivet or rack in the slow cooker, and pour water around the base of the trivet.

Cover and heat on a high setting for 2 to 3 hours.

Fortune's Fool

Serves 4

½ cup orange, lime, or lemon juice
3 tablespoons sugar
3 tablespoons unsalted butter
1 large egg, beaten
2 (3"-long, ½" wide) strips of citrus zest, minced
½ cup heavy cream

Place the juice in a small saucepan. Over medium-high heat, reduce the liquid by half.

Remove the pan from the heat and stir in the sugar and butter. Stir in the egg until well combined.

Return the pan to the burner and cook on medium-low heat for 3 to 5 minutes or until bubbles just begin to form.

Remove the pan from the heat and stir in the citrus zest. Place the pan in a bowl of ice and stir the mixture until it is cold.

In another bowl, whip the cream until stiff. Fold the citrus mixture thoroughly into the cream.

Love at First Bite

Count Orlock's Coconut Pie

Serves 8

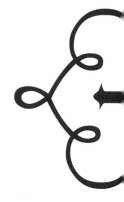

¾ stick of butter, melted
4 eggs
2 cups milk
½ cup flour
¾ cup sugar
1½ teaspoons vanilla
1 cup sweetened shredded coconut

Preheat oven to 350°F. Grease and flour a 10" pie pan.

Place all of the ingredients in a blender and blend for 1 minute. Pour the batter into the prepared pan.

Bake for 45 minutes or until golden on top.

TASTY TIDBIT

WHILE THE POWER OF MOONLIGHT IS MORE CLOSELY ASSOCIATED WITH WEREWOLVES, AND IS PRIMARILY USED IN FILM AND FICTION AS A MATTER OF CREATING AMBIANCE, IT HAS PLAYED A FACTOR IN BRINGING VAMPIRES TO LIFE. IN JOHN POLIDORI'S NOVEL *THE VAMPYRE*, LORD RUTHVEN IS REANIMATED AFTER HE GAVE THE ORDER THAT HIS CORPSE "BE EXPOSED TO THE FIRST COLD RAY OF THE MOON THAT ROSE AFTER HIS DEATH." NO DOUBT THIS GIVES NEW MEANING TO THE TERM "MOON WALK."

True Blood Bread Pudding

Serves 6–8

3–4 cups cubed panettone, toasted
3 cups half-and-half
6 large eggs
4 large egg yolks
½ cup sugar
1 teaspoon vanilla or rum extract
1 cup heavy cream
2 tablespoons Marsala or orange liqueur

Preheat oven to 325°F. Butter a 9" × 13" baking dish and lay the cubed panettone in the dish.

In a large saucepan, blend the half-and-half, eggs, yolks, sugar, and vanilla or rum extract. Whisk and cook over medium heat for about 10 to 15 minutes, then pour over the bread. Bake in a water bath for about 50 to 60 minutes or until a knife inserted in the middle of the pudding comes out clean.

Whip the cream until it has very soft peaks. Stir in the liqueur and spoon over the individual servings of the bread pudding.

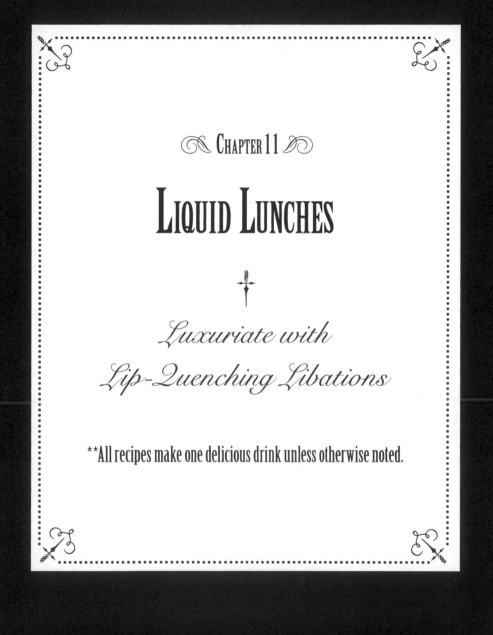

Chapter 11

Liquid Lunches

Luxuriate with
Lip-Quenching Libations

**All recipes make one delicious drink unless otherwise noted.

Barnabas Collins

1½ ounces gin
2 ounces sweet-and-sour mix
Club soda to fill
Orange slice and cherry

Combine gin and sweet-and-sour mix in a shaker. Shake and strain into a Collins glass of ice. Fill with club soda. Garnish with an orange and cherry.

Beautiful Disaster

1 ounce cognac
1 ounce Grand Marnier

Pour ingredients into a brandy snifter and serve.

Berry Bordello

1 ounce strawberry vodka
½ ounce raspberry vodka
½ ounce raspberry liqueur
Cranberry juice to fill
Strawberries and blackberries for garnish

Pour the first three ingredients into a tall glass of ice. Fill with cranberry juice and stir. Garnish with berries.

Black Death

½ ounce black vodka
½ ounce black sambuca
½ ounce Jägermeister

Shake and strain into a shot glass.

Black Magic

2 ounces Blavod black vodka
½ ounce grenadine
7-Up to fill
Maraschino cherry

Pour vodka and grenadine into a tall glass of ice. Fill with 7-Up and stir. Garnish with a maraschino cherry.

Black Martini

1 ounce Blavod black vodka
1 ounce raspberry liqueur
1 ounce triple sec
2 ounces sweet-and-sour mix

Pour all ingredients into a shaker tin of ice. Shake and strain into a martini glass. This black drink looks nice with a white sugared rim.

Black Mojito

5 blackberries
3 sprigs of mint (one for a garnish)
½ fresh lime, chopped
1 ounce simple syrup
1½ ounces light rum
Club soda to fill

Muddle the blackberries, 2 mint sprigs, lime, and simple syrup in a mixing glass. Add the rum. Shake in a shaker tin of ice. Strain into a highball glass of cracked ice. Fill with club soda. Garnish with a mint sprig.

Black Thorn

1 ounce Irish whiskey
1 ounce dry vermouth
3 dashes Pernod
3 dashes bitters

Pour ingredients into a shaker with ice. Stir and strain into a short glass of ice.

Blood Orange Mimosa

Blood orange soda
Champagne
Strawberry half for garnish

Fill a champagne flute one third of the way with blood orange soda then add champagne to fill. Garnish the rim with the strawberry half.

Bloody Beer

2 ounces Bloody Mary mix
14 ounces lager
Dash Tabasco sauce
Dash Worcestershire sauce

Pour the Bloody Mary mix into the beer. Embellish with a dash of Tabasco and a dash of Worcestershire if you like.

Bloody Maria

2 ounces aged tequila
Bloody Mary mix to fill
Celery and lime wedge

Pour the tequila into a tall glass of ice. Fill with Bloody Mary mix. Stir. Garnish with celery and a lime wedge.

Bloody Mary

2 ounces vodka
Bloody Mary mix to fill
Celery stalk
Lime wedge

Combine vodka and mix; stir with ice. Strain into a tall glass filled with ice. Garnish with a stick of celery and lime wedge.

Blow Your Skull Off

1 ounce rum
15 ounces stout
Dash cayenne pepper
Lime slice

Pour the rum into the stout. Sprinkle the cayenne pepper in and mix gently. Squeeze the juice from the lime and drop into the beer.

Brain Hemorrhage

1 ounce peach schnapps
¼ ounce Irish cream
¼ ounce grenadine syrup

First, pour the peach schnapps into a shot glass. Slowly add the Irish cream, and it will clump and settle at the bottom. Next, slowly pour grenadine to give it a bloody, disgusting brain-hemorrhage look.

Burning Love

1 ounce raspberry rum or vodka
1 ounce hazelnut liqueur
½ ounce raspberry liqueur
2 scoops banana ice cream
Milk to blend
Half a banana
1 ounce 151 rum

Put the raspberry rum or vodka, hazelnut liqueur, raspberry liqueur, and banana ice cream into a blender. Add the milk little by little to reach a smooth consistency. Pour into a tall glass and stick the banana into the glass standing up. Pour the 151 rum all over the banana and light.

Captain's Blood

1½ ounces dark rum
¼ ounce lime juice
¼ ounce simple syrup
2 dashes angostura bitters
Lemon peel spiral

Shake all liquid ingredients with ice. Strain into a short glass of ice. Garnish with a spiral of lemon peel.

Champagne Louis

1 ounce gin
1 ounce dry vermouth
⅛ ounce Pernod
Chilled dry champagne to fill
Lemon twist

Shake the gin, vermouth, and Pernod with ice. Strain into a champagne flute. Fill with champagne and add a lemon twist.

Cocoa Carfax

1 teaspoon sugar
½ teaspoon cinnamon powder
1 ounce Irish cream
1 packet hot cocoa
Hot water to fill
Whipped cream or miniature marshmallows (optional)

Mix the sugar and cinnamon together on a saucer. Wet the rim of a mug and dip it in the cinnamon-sugar mix. Pour the Irish cream and the cocoa into the mug. Fill with hot water and stir. Garnish with whipped cream or mini marshmallows.

Coconut Coronary

1 ounce coconut rum
1 ounce vanilla vodka
1 ounce Coco Lopez
Pineapple juice and orange juice to fill
Splash of grenadine

Pour the first three ingredients into a tall glass of ice. Fill with the juices. Splash in the grenadine. Stir.

Collinwood Cocktail

2 ounces rye whiskey
Juice of half a lemon
½ ounce simple syrup
Club soda to fill
Orange slice and cherry

Shake the first three ingredients. Strain into a Collins glass of ice. Fill with club soda and garnish with an orange and cherry.

Corpse Reviver

1 ounce gin
½ ounce Cointreau
½ ounce Lillet Blanc
¾ ounce fresh lemon juice
¼ ounce absinthe

Shake all ingredients with ice. Strain into a martini glass.

Damsel in Distress

1 fresh lime, peeled and chopped
Loose handful of blueberries
1½ ounces damson gin

Muddle the chopped fresh lime and blueberries in a rocks glass. Add the damson gin, stir, and top up with crushed ice.

Dark 'n Stormy Night

2 ounces Gosling's dark rum
Ginger beer to fill
Lime wedge

Pour the rum over ice in a highball glass and fill with ginger beer. Squeeze in a lime wedge.

Deadly Affair

1 ounce strawberry schnapps
1 ounce cranberry juice
1 ounce orange juice

Pour all ingredients into an ice-filled mixing glass. Stir well, then strain into a cocktail glass.

Death by Chocolatini

½ ounce chocolate
Strawberry
Chocolate syrup
1½ ounces vanilla vodka
1½ ounces chocolate liqueur
2 ounces cream

Melt the chocolate in a microwave; then dip the strawberry in the chocolate. Cool in the freezer. Swirl chocolate syrup inside a martini glass. Set the martini glass in the freezer. Pour the vodka, liqueur, and cream into a shaker tin. Shake, then strain into the chilled glass. Garnish the rim with the chocolate-covered strawberry.

Death in the Afternoon

1 ounce absinthe
Chilled champagne to fill

Pour absinthe into a champagne flute. Fill with champagne.

Devil's Blood

¾ glass cranberry juice
2 ounces Blavod black vodka

Pack a tall glass with ice; then pour the cranberry juice three-quarters to the top. Slowly pour the black vodka on top.

Diablo Cocktail

1 ounce brandy
1 ounce dry vermouth
1 ounce Cointreau
Dash angostura bitters
Dash Regans' orange bitters

Combine ingredients in a shaker
half filled with ice. Shake well.
Strain into a cocktail glass.

Drac's Dirty Girl

1 ounce vodka
1 ounce coffee liqueur
1 ounce Irish cream liqueur
¼ ounce green crème de menthe

Combine ingredients in a shaker
half filled with ice. Shake well.
Strain into an old-fashioned glass
with ice.

Dusk 'til Dawn

¾ ounce light rum
½ ounce lemon juice
¾ ounce brandy
¾ ounce triple sec
Lemon twist

Pour all liquids into shaker. Shake
with ice. Strain into a martini
glass. Garnish with a lemon twist.

El Diablo

2 ounces aged tequila
¾ ounce crème de cassis
Ginger ale to fill

Pour the tequila and crème de
cassis into a highball glass of ice.
Fill with ginger ale.

Elixir of Life

1 ounce Parfait Amour
1 ounce raspberry vodka
White cranberry juice and club
soda to fill

Pour Parfait Amour and vodka
into a tall glass of ice. Fill with
equal parts of white cranberry
juice and club soda.

Fallen Angel

1 ounce amaretto
½ ounce gin
½ ounce vodka
½ ounce 151 rum
½ ounce dark rum
1 ounce grenadine
Cranberry, pineapple, and grapefruit juice to fill

Pour the liquors and grenadine
into a tall glass of ice. Fill with
equal parts cranberry, pineapple,
and grapefruit juice.

Femme Fatale

½ ounce pineapple vodka
1 ounce pineapple juice
Champagne to fill

Shake the vodka and pineapple juice. Strain into a champagne flute. Fill with champagne.

First Kiss

1½ ounces coconut rum
1½ ounces pineapple juice
1 ounce milk
¼ ounce grenadine

Shake ingredients with ice. Strain into a chilled martini glass.

Flame in My Heart

½ ounce Dooley's Toffee Liqueur
½ ounce coffee liqueur
¾ ounce Grand Marnier
Reese's Peanut Butter Cup

Pour the toffee liqueur, coffee liqueur, and ½ ounce of Grand Marnier in a shot glass.

Take a spoon and scoop out a little of the middle of the peanut butter cup. Eat the middle and set the rest on top of the shot glass.

Flame in My Heart (cont'd)

Pour in the remaining ¼ ounce of Grand Marnier into the scooped out area and light.

When the flame dies, drink the shot and eat the candy.

Fog Cutter

2 ounces white rum
1 ounce brandy
½ ounce gin
2 ounces fresh lemon juice
1 ounce fresh orange juice
½ ounce orgeat syrup
½ ounce sweet sherry

Shake everything but the sherry with ice. Strain into a tall glass of ice. Float the sherry on top.

Foggy Afternoon

1 ounce vodka
½ ounce apricot brandy
½ ounce triple sec
1¼ ounces crème de banana
1¼ ounces fresh lemon juice

Shake all ingredients with ice. Strain into a martini glass.

Forbidden Fruit

1 ounce spiced rum
1 ounce apple schnapps
¼ ounce cinnamon schnapps
7-Up to fill

Pour the first three ingredients into a glass of ice. Fill with 7-Up.

Gin and Sin

2 ounces gin
¼ ounce fresh lemon juice
¼ ounce orange juice
¼ ounce grenadine

Shake all ingredients in a shaker of ice. Strain into a martini glass.

Ginger Snap

2 ounces tequila
Schweppes green tea ginger ale to fill

Pour the tequila into a highball glass of ice. Fill with green tea ginger ale.

Green-Eyed Goddess

1 ounce melon liqueur
1 ounce Irish cream
1 ounce banana liqueur
2 ounces cream or milk

Green-Eyed Goddess (cont'd)

Pour all ingredients into a shaker of ice. Shake and strain into a cocktail glass.

Hair-Raising Southern Hospitality

2 ounces Southern Comfort
2 ounces peach schnapps

Fill a shaker tin with ice and add the Southern Comfort and peach schnapps. Shake for about 20 seconds. Strain into a cocktail glass.

Hot Blooded

1½ ounces tequila
Several dashes Tabasco
⅛ ounce 151 rum

Pour the tequila into a shot glass and add dashes of Tabasco. Gently layer the 151 rum on top, then light. Allow the flame to die, then drink.

Howl at the Moon

1 ounce coffee liqueur
1 ounce amaretto
2 ounces Irish cream (optional)

Pour ingredients into a shaker. Shake and pour into a short glass of ice. Cream can be added if desired.

Hypnotizing Margarita

Kosher salt
1½ ounces aged tequila
1 ounce Hpnotiq
Lime juice from half a lime
3 ounces sweet-and-sour mix
Lime wedge

Rim a margarita glass with salt. Pour the tequila, Hpnotiq, lime juice, and sweet-and-sour mix in a blender with a cup of ice and blend. Pour into the glass and garnish with lime wedge.

Kiss from a Rosarita

Kosher salt
1½ ounces aged tequila
1 ounce Tequila Rose
3 ounces sweet-and-sour mix
3 strawberries
Lime wheel

Rim a margarita glass with salt. Put the liquid ingredients and the strawberries in a blender with a cup of ice and blend. Pour into the glass and garnish with a lime wedge.

Love Potion #9

1 ounce mandarin vodka
1 ounce Parfait Amor
White (clear) cranberry juice to fill
Sprig of purple seedless grapes

Pour vodka and Parfait Amour into a tall glass of ice. Fill with white cranberry juice. Garnish with the grapes.

Man Hunter

1½ ounces Wild Turkey 101
1 ounce curaçao
½ ounce sweet vermouth
½ ounce fresh lemon juice

Shake all ingredients with ice. Strain into a martini glass.

Mai Tai Me Up

1 ounce dark rum
½ ounce light rum
1 ounce pineapple juice
1 ounce fresh lemon juice
½ ounce simple syrup
1 slice canned pineapple
Maraschino cherry

Shake first five ingredients in a cocktail shaker with ice. Strain in a martini glass Garnish with pineapple and cherry.

Mistress of Death

1 ounce melon liqueur
1 ounce lemon vodka or rum
7-Up to fill
Maraschino cherry

Pour melon liqueur and vodka or rum into a tall glass of ice. Fill with 7-Up and stir. Garnish with a maraschino cherry.

Moonlight Drive

1 ounce vodka
1 ounce rum
1 ounce sloe gin
1 ounce coconut rum
½ ounce amaretto
Orange and pineapple juice to fill

Pour the liquors into a tall glass of ice. Fill with juices.

My Bloody Valentine

4 ounces Beaujolais
2 ounces cranberry juice

Combine ingredients in a shaker half filled with ice. Shake, then strain into a wine glass.

My Freaky Valentine

1 ounce Shakers Rose Vodka
1 ounce Tequila Rose strawberry cream liqueur
2 ounces cream

Shake all ingredients with ice and strain into a martini glass.

Painkiller

2 ounces Pusser's rum
4 ounces piña colada mix
1 ounce fresh orange juice
Sprinkle of nutmeg

Blend first three ingredients with ice. Pour into a tropical glass. Sprinkle with nutmeg.

Pale Lady

1½ ounces Plymouth Gin
¾ ounce Cointreau
¾ ounce fresh lemon juice
Lemon twist

Shake with ice. Strain into a chilled martini glass. Garnish with a lemon twist.

Passion Beer

14 ounces light beer
½ ounce passion fruit juice
1 ounce passion liqueur

Pour all ingredients into a glass. Gently mix.

Passion Cup

2 ounces vodka
2 ounces orange juice
1 ounce passion fruit juice
½ ounce coconut cream
Maraschino cherry

Combine liquid ingredients in a shaker half filled with ice. Shake well. Strain into a large wine glass. Top with a cherry.

Red Death

¾ ounce vodka
¾ ounce Southern Comfort
¼ ounce sloe gin
¼ ounce triple sec
¼ ounce Rose's lime juice
¼ ounce grenadine
Orange juice to fill

Pour liquors and grenadine into a tall glass of ice. Fill with orange juice.

Red Eye

2 ounces tomato juice
14 ounces lager

Pour the tomato juice into the beer.

Renfield's Frog in a Blender Delight

1 ounce coffee liqueur
1 ounce green crème de menthe
2 ounces cream
½ ounce red cinnamon schnapps

Put a cup of ice into a blender. Pour in the first three ingredients and blend. Pour into a tall glass and add the red cinnamon schnapps on top. This drink can also be shaken and strained into a cocktail glass.

Rosy Red Cheeks
Yields about 6 cups

2 cups cranberry juice cocktail
1 (6-ounce) can frozen orange juice concentrate
1 tablespoon sugar
¼ teaspoon ground allspice
1 bottle dry red wine
1 orange
10 whole cloves
Red food coloring

Rosy Red Cheeks (cont'd)

Combine the cranberry juice, orange juice concentrate, sugar, allspice, and wine in the slow cooker. Cover and heat on a low setting for 2 to 3 hours. Slice the orange and stud the orange slices with the cloves. Half an hour before serving, put the orange slices in the slow cooker. Add a few drops of red food coloring for extra bloody color.

Rusty Nail in the Coffin

1½ ounces Scotch
½ ounce Drambuie

Pour ingredients into a short glass of ice.

Satan's Whiskers

¾ ounce gin
¾ ounce dry vermouth
½ ounce Grand Marnier
¾ ounce sweet vermouth
½ ounce orange juice
2 dashes orange bitters

Shake all ingredients with ice. Strain into a martini glass.

Screaming Banshee

1 ounce banana liqueur
1 ounce white crème de cacao
2 ounces cream

Combine ingredients in a shaker. Shake, then pour into a cocktail glass.

Shady Lady

1 ounce blanco tequila
1 ounce melon liqueur
Fresh pink grapefruit juice to fill

Pour the tequila and melon liqueur into a highball glass of ice. Fill with grapefruit juice.

Silk Stalking

2 ounces aged tequila
1 ounce Chambord
1 ounce crème de cacao
1 ounce cream

Combine and shake all ingredients with ice. Strain into a martini glass.

Sinister Southern Lady

2 ounces bourbon
1 ounce Southern Comfort
1 ounce amaretto
3 ounces pineapple juice
Sprite or 7-Up to fill

Pour the first four ingredients into a tall glass of ice. Fill with Sprite or 7-Up.

Snake Bite

2 ounces Yukon Jack
½ ounce Rose's lime juice

Shake and strain into a large shot, shooter, or rocks glass.

Spontaneous Combustion

2 ounces aged tequila
1 ounce fresh lime juice
1 ounce honey
2 dashes Regan's orange bitters

Combine and shake all ingredients with ice. Strain into a martini glass.

Succulent Sunset

1½ ounces orange-flavored vodka
½ ounce grenadine
Orange juice to fill
Orange slice

Fill a tall glass with ice. Pour in the orange-flavored vodka and the grenadine. Slowly fill the glass with orange juice. The result will be a red layer on the bottom mixing with the orange layer. Garnish with an orange slice.

Tequila Sunrise

1½ ounces blanco tequila
½ ounce grenadine
Fresh orange juice to fill

Pour the tequila and grenadine into a highball glass of ice. Fill with fresh orange juice.

Tequila Sunrise Margarita

Kosher salt
1½ ounces blanco tequila
½ ounce triple sec
½ ounce grenadine
1 ounce orange juice
1 ounce sweet-and-sour mix
Lime wedge

Love at First Bite

Tequila Sunrise Margarita (cont'd)

Rim a margarita glass with salt. Pour liquid ingredients into a blender with a cup of ice and blend. Pour into the glass and garnish with a lime wedge.

Thirst Quencher

10 ounces light beer
5 ounces limeade
1 ounce gin

Combine the beer, gin, and limeade. Stir gently to mix.

Vampire Bite

2 ounces aged tequila
1/4 ounce triple sec
1/4 ounce Drambuie
2 ounces lemon juice
1/2 teaspoon sugar
Dash bitters

Shake all ingredients with ice. Strain into a martini glass.

Walk in the Moonlight

1 ounce black tequila
1 ounce black vodka
1 ounce lime juice
1 ounce simple syrup

Combine and shake all ingredients with ice. Strain into a martini glass.

Wicked Witch's Socks

1/3 ounce coffee liqueur
1/3 ounce white crème de cacao
1/3 ounce black vodka

Into a shot glass, layer each ingredient in order with a spoon.

Zombie

1 ounce light rum
1 ounce dark rum
1 ounce apricot brandy
1/2 ounce 151 float
Bar punch mix to fill
Orange slice and cherry

Combine all liquid ingredients and shake with ice. Strain into a tall glass of ice. Garnish with an orange slice and cherry.

MOCKTAILS

Here are some maniacal mixed drinks that will help you keep your wits about you.

Bone Chiller

Half a peeled cucumber
Juice from half a lime
Half a peeled ripe kiwi
1 tablespoon sugar
1 ounce water
Sprig of mint

Put all ingredients except mint in a blender. Add ice until you reach a frozen yet pourable consistency. Pour into a martini glass and garnish with mint.

Hellmouth Mimosa

2 ounces fresh orange juice
Chilled sparkling white grape juice to fill

Pour orange juice into a champagne flute. Fill with sparkling white grape juice.

Sweet Tart

Handful of blackberries
1 teaspoon sugar or sweetener
Lemonade to fill
Lemon slice and blackberries

Blend the blackberries and sugar or sweetener in a blender until mixed well. Pour into a tall glass. Fill the glass with lemonade and ice. Garnish with a lemon slice and some blackberries.

Twilight Party Punch

2 ounces pineapple juice
3 ounces fresh orange juice
1 ounce fresh lemon juice
½ ounce grenadine
Fruit

Combine all liquid ingredients in a shaker half filled with ice. Shake well. Strain into a tall glass of ice. Garnish with your favorite fruit.

Love at First Bite

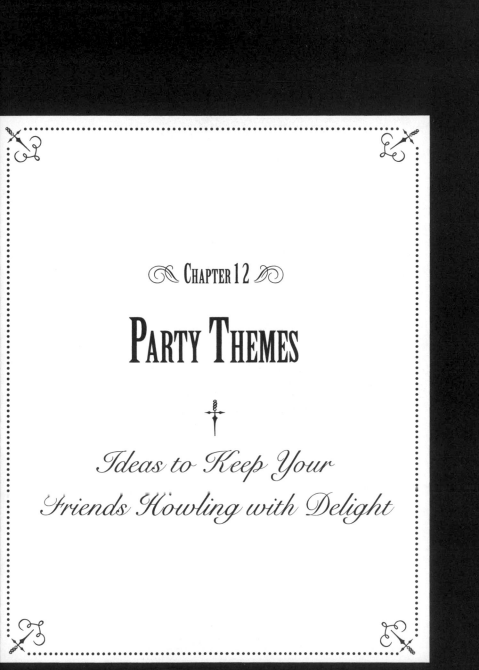

CHAPTER 12

PARTY THEMES

Ideas to Keep Your Friends Howling with Delight

Party at Twilight

Get your girlfriends together for a fun-filled evening with Bella, Edward, and Jacob as the guests of honor. Get comfortable on the couch and have a private screening of *Twilight* while snacking on some of these tantalizing tidbits.

Italian Cheese Flight Delight (page 25)
Jaw-Snapping Sausage Bites (page 29)
Bella's Favorite Mushroom Ravioli (page 204)
Edward's Sparkle Cake (page 224)
Twilight Party Punch (page 260)

Vampire Must-See TV Party

There are some truly fangtastic vampire themed television shows out there. Whether you are devoted to *True Blood*, *The Vampire Diaries*, or an old favorite like *Buffy the Vampire Slayer*, you can sink your teeth into some great episodes while gnawing on sinfully good snacks. Some other shows worth checking out on TV or DVD are *Blood Ties*, *Supernatural*, *Angel*, *Vampire High*, *Moonlight*, *Blade*, and *Dark Shadows*. Whatever you want to watch, do it while sinking your teeth into the following tantalizing treats:

Deviled Eggs (page 14)
Beaten and Bruised Brie and Blue Spread (page 16)
Fruit Bat Pizza Bites (page 23)
Killer Chili (page 38)
Sookie's Shrimp Scampi Kababs (page 90)
Angel's Strawberry Cake (page 231)
Barnabus Collins (page 246)
Sinister Southern Lady (page 258)

Love at First Bite

Haunted Halloween Party

Ah, the favorite holiday of the undead. A night to match all nights. Dress as your favorite character and start dancing the Monster Mash.

Bloody Mary Aspic and Eggs (page 21)
Blood Bowl (page 47)
Buffalo Bat Wings (page 122)
Chopped to Bits Salad (page 56)
Finger Sandwiches (page 81)
Vlad's Veggie Quesadillas (page 208)
Lady's Fingers (page 232)
Cat Tongues (page 217)
Coffin Cake (page 218)
Spider Bites (page 238)
Rosy Red Cheeks (page 256)

TASTY TIDBIT

AND WHAT HORRIFIC HALLOWEEN PARTY WOULD BE COMPLETE WITHOUT A BANK OF BLOOD TO LURE IN YOUR VAMPIRE FRIENDS? HERE IS AN EASY WAY TO MAKE A STASH OF YOUR OWN. COMBINE 1 CUP KARO SYRUP, 1 TABLESPOON WATER, 2 TABLESPOONS RED FOOD COLORING, AND 1 TEASPOON YELLOW FOOD COLORING IN A MIXING BOWL OR CAULDRON. YOU CAN ADJUST THE AMOUNTS AND EVEN ADD SOME DISH SOAP TO GET THE COLOR AND CONSISTENCY YOU DESIRE.

Red Carpet Picture Show

Choose your favorite vampire movie, send out fancy invitations, and ask your guests to dress in their finest garb for a red carpet viewing at your place. Here is a list of some suggested flicks.

Blade (1998) Wesley Snipes, Stephen Dorff, Kris Kristofferson

Bram Stoker's Dracula (1992) Gary Oldman, Anthony Hopkins, Winona Ryder

Buffy the Vampire Slayer (1992) Kristy Swanson, Donald Sutherland, Rutger Hauer

Cirque du Freak: The Vampire's Assistant (2009) John C. Reilly, Josh Hutcherson, Chris Massoglia

Dracula (1931) Bela Lugosi, Helen Chandler, David Manners, Edward Van Sloan

Dracula 2000 (2000) Gerard Butler, Christopher Plummer, Jonny Lee Miller, Justine Waddell

Dracula vs. Frankenstein (1971) J. Carrol Naish, Lon Chaney Jr., Zandor Vorkov

Eclipse (2010) Kristen Stewart, Robert Pattinson, Taylor Lautner

From Dusk till Dawn (1996) Harvey Keitel, George Clooney, Quentin Tarantino

Interview with the Vampire: The Vampire Chronicles (1994) Tom Cruise, Brad Pitt, Kirsten Dunst

John Carpenter's Vampires (1998) James Woods, Daniel Baldwin, Sheryl Lee

The Lost Boys (1987) Jason Patric, Corey Haim, Kiefer Sutherland

Love at First Bite (1979) George Hamilton, Susan Saint James

New Moon (2009) Kristen Stewart, Robert Pattinson, Taylor Lautner

Nosferatu (1922, German) Max Schreck

Once Bitten (1985) Lauren Hutton, Jim Carrey, Cleavon Little

Salem's Lot (1979) David Soul, James Mason, Lance Kerwin

Shadow of the Vampire (2000) Willem Dafoe, John Malkovich, Cary Elwes

30 Days of Night (2007) Josh Hartnett, Melissa George, Danny Huston

Twilight (2008) Kristen Stewart, Robert Pattinson, Taylor Lautner

Ultraviolet (2006) Milla Jovovich, Cameron Bright, Nick Chinlund

Underworld (2003) Kate Beckinsale, Scott Speedman, Michael Sheen, Bill Nighy

Underworld: Evolution (2006) Kate Beckinsale, Scott Speedman, Tony Curran

Van Helsing (2004) Hugh Jackman, Kate Beckinsale

INDEX